"Dr. Manning has dedicated his time, through years of research, to helping develop athletes' minds to reach greater accomplishments and capabilities in not only their sports but in their daily lives. I have complete confidence in what he has taught me. Through countless hours of mentoring and coaching, I have become the player I am today and can only expect better accomplishments to come!"

 —James Ludlow, Professional Tennis Player

"Learning Craig Manning's insights into the world of sports psychology has helped me to develop techniques and life skills vital to performance on and off the ski hill. His coaching is key to helping me limit interference; elevate confidence, concentration, and motivation; and free my mind to become a fearless and successful athlete and human being. My personal experience of life and sports has taken on a new level of fulfillment, balance, and success."

 —Emily Cook, US Olympic Team

"The skills I learned from this book helped me go from being a mediocre college athlete to one of the top three jumpers in NCAA."

 —Bobby Low, NCAA All-American, Professional Athlete,
  Track and Field

Denice

Thank you for sharing
you gift of leadership with
all.

Craig Manning

For my wife, McKenzie

THE
FEARLESS
MIND

5

Essential Steps to
Higher Performance

CRAIG MANNING, PhD

CFI
Springville, Utah

ISBN 13: 978-1-59955-396-2

Published by CFI, an imprint of Cedar Fort, Inc., 2373 W. 700 S., Springville, UT 84663
Distributed by Cedar Fort, Inc., www.cedarfort.com

Library of Congress Cataloging-in-Publication Data

    Manning, Craig, 1970-
     The fearless mind / Craig Manning.
      p. cm.
     ISBN 978-1-59955-396-2 (acid-free paper)
     1. Success. 2. Fear. 3. Self-realization. I. Title.

    BF637.S8M283 2010
    158.1--dc22

    2009048062

Cover design by Megan Whittier
Cover design © 2009 by Lyle Mortimer
Edited and typeset by Kimiko M. Hammari

Printed in the United States of America

10 9 8 7 6 5 4 3 2 1

Printed on acid-free paper

Contents

THE JOURNEY OF LIFE

Introduction

"Not I—not anyone else can travel that road for you,
You must travel it for yourself."
—Walt Whitman[1]

IN TODAY'S MULTITASKING, TEXT-MESSAGING, HIGHLY SOPHISTICATED world, the pressure to perform is greater than ever. That being said, when all things are equal—which they invariably are, thanks to modern-day technology—the mentally tough athlete, the businessperson, or the homemaker who has learned to harness the strength of the mind wins every time. Hence, this book is about learning to gain greater control over our minds to channel our energy in more productive ways. Life is a performance, whether we are on a court, in an office, running a home, or simply spending quality time with our children. We are always performing. If we control our minds, we can make our lives fulfilling.

Growing up in Australia, I loved playing sports of all kinds. I wasn't too interested in school and would get my homework done as quickly as possible to allow for more playing time. In my early teens, I realized I needed to focus on a particular sport if I was to try to make a career of it. I thought tennis would probably be my best bet. Although tennis was probably the sport at which I was the least skilled, I liked it the most, and I had an infrastructure within my family that greatly helped me improve my game (my dad was a great tennis player, my uncle was a coach by profession, and my cousin was very good and would later play professionally). I chose to channel all my attention on tennis.

I worked hard on my game and improved quickly. By the time I was almost eighteen, I decided to give it a go on the professional tennis tour. This really doesn't mean much; anyone can play pro tournaments at any point in time. All you have to do is sign up and pay the entry fee. I got accepted onto a private team made up of young Australian hopefuls. We traveled throughout Europe for nearly six months playing in tournaments, and I played in every pro tournament in Australia throughout the year.

My ultimate objective was to become the best tennis player in the world. However, from the time I was very young, I have always been a deep thinker, analyzing things, breaking things down, and trying to understand how everything works. I often pondered questions like, "Why do people do what they do?" or "Why do some people perform so well while others struggle?" I could never seem to shut off my mind. At times this was a major challenge, especially on the tennis court, and it resulted in more than my fair share of dismal performances. At other times, it was a great benefit, like when I persevered and completed a PhD in sports psychology. When I look back now, I realize a career as a professional tennis player wasn't in the cards for me.

But it was not until I was traveling through Europe playing pro tournaments that I realized I didn't enjoy tennis. You would think that traveling the world, living in a different city or even a different country from one week to the next would be a great way to live, but it just didn't suit me. I didn't enjoy living out of a suitcase, but more important, at the time, my mind was far from a fearless one.

My parents were footing the bill for my traveling experience, and I couldn't bear to see them sacrificing so much on the slight chance I might make it as a professional tennis player. It is a tough, grueling life trying to make a living on the pro tour. The third year I stayed home while my mates went back on tour. It was a bit of a rough year. I had always been so driven, but now I found myself careerless, jobless, and without much of anything to my name.

Tennis had been who I was; it had been my identity. Through high school I was known as Craig the tennis player. Without it I became lost and confused. I would ask questions of those who appeared to know themselves and their purpose in life: "Why do you do this?" "Why do you do that?" Yet I could never get an answer that made much sense to me. When I look back now, I realize I was looking for the deeper or real reasons why some succeed yet many fail. Meanwhile, I did whatever I could to keep myself busy, even completing a tax preparation course so

I could work with my father, who owned his own accounting practice. I worked with my grandfather renovating one of his warehouses and taught tennis lessons. I ended up being very busy, but none of these professions seemed to fill the void inside me. After about six or seven months of running around in circles, the oddest thing happened.

I went away to a small country town tournament with some mates who weren't really high-level tennis players but more social players. I hadn't played for a while, so I was a bit out of shape. The guys I was with recovered quickly from their matches, mainly because they didn't play too much tennis and usually lost pretty early in the tournament. I was good enough to do well at this level of competition and played tennis for two days straight. The combination of sleep deprivation from the silly tents we slept in and being out of match-shape wiped me out.

The day after we got back, I was to teach a tennis camp at the club where I trained while growing up. When I arrived, my mate's father, the owner of the facility, said he wanted me to hit a few balls with a man who was in town for a veteran's tournament. I was not feeling well at all. I had planned on toughing out the day and heading straight home to get some sleep. But since my mate's dad told me this man was in his late forties, I thought, "No worries. I will stand in one place and make him run around; he will be worn out in half an hour or so."

Two and a half hours later, we finally finished. This man was one of those super forty-year-olds who is in better shape at forty than he was in his twenties. Upon completion of our hitting, he asked what I was doing with my life. I told him I was waiting to get into a university later that year. I was planning on studying accounting and working with my dad. He asked me why I didn't use my tennis to get a good education in the States. He said he knew a coach at the tournament he was heading to and that he would be sure to mention me to him.

It wasn't long before I got a phone call from the coach at Brigham Young University (BYU) in Provo, Utah, wanting me to come and play in the States. At the last possible moment I took the opportunity to come to the United States. When I first arrived at BYU, I wasn't sure it was the place for me. I struggled for a while trying to figure out who I was and what I wanted to do with my life. When I finally got my act together (found some harmony and balance within myself), I switched my major to psychology, stopped fighting with myself on the tennis court, and started performing a lot better both on and off the court.

I played four years and then coached as an undergrad assistant with the men's team for a year. After undergraduate studies, I took a job as the women's assistant tennis coach at BYU while working on my master's degree in psychology. I still had many contacts back in Australia and was able to experience some recruiting success. After two successful years of working with the women's program (the program went from being ranked around 25 in the country to a high of 5), I was encouraged to switch to the men's program to help them.

After a year of working full time with the men's program and bringing in a number of solid players, I think the administrators thought I knew what I was doing. After working with the men's team, I was offered the position of head women's tennis coach at BYU. At the time, I was young for a head coach at a Division I institution. The program had fallen on some hard times; they weren't even ranked in the top 75 in the country, despite a strong tradition. While attempting to build the women's program back to what it had been, I started working on my PhD in sports psychology at the University of Utah in Salt Lake City.

When I first started as the head coach, my philosophy was basically to help the players on the team however I could. Adhering to the belief that hard work was the key to success, we had some early success, taking the team from being unranked to a high of 32 and settling in around the high 30s out of 311 Division I women's tennis programs. We lost in the final of the conference tournament that first year. In the second year we won a conference title, and to this day, I have no idea how we did that, except that we all worked hard.

The third year we had some internal problems. This was a very tough experience, and I learned an awful lot about honesty and self-destructive behavior during this time frame. By the fourth year I was starting to get some of my own players in, but still it wasn't good enough; something wasn't quite right. After this season, I took some time to really think about what we were doing as a team. I had completed my course work by this time for my PhD and was beginning to formulate my own ideas on how to facilitate high performance.

I had been contemplating high performance for as long as I could remember. I felt that what was going on with our tennis team at that time represented what had been going on in my life: I was working hard but not really going anywhere. It felt like we were in a cycle of mediocrity that was leading to feelings of disappointment. In regard to the tennis team, we worked hard on our strokes, footwork, conditioning, and so forth. But what was the point in working so hard, when—under pressure, when it really mattered the most—we consistently underperformed?

Ultimately, I decided to change everything we were doing. I wanted every drill to have a mental purpose to it. I made it mandatory for the players to have a clear objective and a plan to achieve the objective before every match. After matches each player was required to give me feedback on what they did well and what they wanted to improve. My father-in-law, Dr. Scott Baird, had taught me how to inspire accelerated growth. I implemented everything I thought pertinent from my studies and discussions with my father-in-law in an effort to help the team. That was the beginning of developing a fearless mind in the athletes on the team.

I was amazed how the players on the team enjoyed and responded to this process. They more than just enjoyed it; they seemed to crave it. Evaluating our own performance and trying to make it better feels good; it feels right. Our team went from a totally physical, almost mindless machine that would at times just go through the motions, to this highly alert, attuned-to-the-reality-of-the-moment group of individuals working toward individual perfection, united with a common purpose.

Although each year there are always variables that have an effect on the performance of the team, this is what the statistics showed after that fourth year. Before we made the switch from a purely physical approach, we had a record of 12–11, a 52 percent win percentage against opponents with an average national rank of 25. Upon implementing the "mental model," we went 22–6, a 78 percent win percentage against opponents with an average rank of 23.5. The following year we went 22–4, an 84 percent win percentage against opponents with an average rank of 34. That was a 32 percent increase in wins over just two seasons.

Every player we had on our team improved their win percentage in subsequent years. I have even broken it down into the first half of the year compared to the second. Because our system is cognitive in nature, it takes a little time for people to get it down. This is evidenced by the greater win percentage in our players in the second half of the season compared to the first half of the season.

In summary, the classical model of performance is potential (innate physical skills) plus training (physical advancements in speed and agility) equals performance (PO + T = P). This model is not just out of date; it never was adequate in the first place. To me, the performance model is potential plus training minus interference equals high performance (PO + T − I = HP).

I believe we all have potential to do great things. We may not be successful in every area of our lives, but if we follow our heart, we can all find our niche. If that niche is athletics, then getting into and staying in great physical condition is a must, not an advantage. Although potential plus training are critical, they only get you into the game. Playing the game at the highest levels of our ability comes down to how well we have learned to control our minds, to rid ourselves of any and all interference, and to stay focused on what needs to be done. If we allow interference into our psyche, it doesn't matter how much potential we have or how hard we train; we will not be able to make our dreams come true.

The following chapters of this book explain how to develop a fearless mind and set ourselves and those around us up for success while avoiding cycles of mediocrity that rob us of all that we could be.

Note
1. Walt Whitman, "Song of Myself," *Leaves of Grass* (New York: Modern Library, 2001), 106.

The Dream

*"No matter how impossible it all may seem . . .
Never underestimate the power of a dream."*
—Author unknown

How many people in this world really care how successful we become? How many people really care how happy we are? I don't mean to sound negative, but really, how many? It is important to be honest with ourselves. This is our life; there is no time to waste with false modesty or humility. Our parents hopefully care. What about our grandparents? I believe they do. How about our siblings or friends? What about our coaches or teachers? Do they really care how happy we are?

Many people want to see us do well, but they have their own responsibilities, their own lives to live, and their own dreams to fulfill. For the most part, they are not staying up late worrying about whether we win our tennis match or get into grad school. The reality is, no one can make our dreams come true for us. Although it seems many parents fight this battle at times, we have to do it for ourselves.

Internationally acclaimed spiritual teacher Marianne Williamson once said:

> Our deepest fear is not that we are inadequate. Our deepest fear is that we are powerful beyond measure. It is our light, not our darkness, that most frightens us. We ask ourselves, WHO am I to be brilliant, gorgeous, talented, fabulous? Actually, who are you *not* to be? You are a child of God. Your playing small doesn't serve the world. There's nothing enlightened about shrinking so that other people won't feel insecure around you. We are all meant to shine, as

children do. We were born to make manifest the glory of God that is within us. It's not just in some of us; it's in everyone. And as we let our own light shine, we unconsciously give other people permission to do the same. As we're liberated from our own fear, our presence automatically liberates others.[1]

Our dreams need to remain exactly that—ours. If we truly follow what we love and not what we like, what is safe and easy, or what someone else wants us to do, we will have more passion and energy; we will achieve higher levels of performance; and we will find greater joy. This passion for life will spill over onto those with whom we come in contact—our families, friends, and coworkers. I truly believe that if we have the fearlessness to follow our hearts, there is not much we cannot do. Those who don't follow their hearts never find true happiness, for happiness cannot be given; we must find it for ourselves.

I coached a highly ranked senior tennis player (I will call her Elise) who had great skill sets and a tremendous knowledge of the game. Elise aspired to play tennis professionally after her college days. However, early in her senior year, she didn't win a match and perceived it as a bad loss. She gave up on her aspirations to become a professional tennis player. From this point she struggled to win a match, constantly battling with herself. I have seen this happen several times. When we don't have a clear objective or dream that is ours, all the skill and knowledge in the world will not help us.

Thomas Henry Huxley once wrote, "The great end of life is not knowledge but action."[2] I love this quote because to me it sums up the purpose of our existence. Our actions define us. At the "great end," what do we want to look back on and remember—a fearless life really lived, or a fearful life? When all is said and done, we are responsible for what we did with the time that was given to us.

I worry about the time I have wasted, when I have allowed my mind to swim around in unproductive ways, because I haven't always had the courage to chase my objectives. I now work to accelerate growth toward the objectives I have set for myself. It is a continuous journey that is becoming more enjoyable as the years pass. There have been objectives achieved along the way that have been celebrated for a time, but the journey continues. I am looking forward to the challenge of seeing what the future holds.

Notes

1. Marianne Williamson, *A Return to Love: Reflections on the Principles of "A Course in Miracles"* (New York: HarperCollins, 1992), 165.
2. Quoted in Anthony Robbins, *Unlimited Power* (New York: Fawcett Columbine, 1986), 3.

A Fearless Mind

"Let nothing perturb you, nothing frighten you.
All things pass;
God does not change.
Patience achieves everything."
      —St. Teresa of Avila[1]

AWHILE BACK, I WAS WORKING WITH a young freshman on our tennis team who has been blessed with great physical skill sets, fast-twitch muscle fiber (explosive in her movements), smooth strokes, and great hand-eye coordination—all the physical skills one could ever need to be a high-performing tennis player. Unfortunately, she also struggles with debilitating self-doubt.

Despite her explosive movements, smooth strokes, and vast playing experience, she (I will call her Linda) struggles at times to even get her serve in the court. I have seen her double-fault games away on several occasions, yet in practice she is a strong performer. Playing loose and relaxed, she is close to the best player on our team. It has taken countless hours to hone her physical skills. In my opinion they are good enough for her to be a top professional tennis player, and she could possibly make millions if she could somehow transfer what she does in practice to matches. Unfortunately, like so many people, she has spent little or no time developing the mental skill sets that protect us from the crippling effects of self-doubt.

In one match Linda was double-faulting her service games away time and time again. On the changeovers her hands were shaking uncontrollably, and her breathing was so heavy I was concerned she was about to have a full-blown panic attack. My heart went out to Linda; she appeared so caught up in feelings of helplessness and a perceived lack of control over her situation. While sitting on the bench watching Linda go through this inner battle, I remember telling myself, "Surely this is not worth it." After all, it was just a tennis match. But she kept on trying. Given the circumstances, it was admirable that she just didn't give up.

I have seen athletes go through this, stuck in a heated battle with themselves, so tied up in knots that their performances in real match situations don't come close to resembling the level of performance in practice—not to mention it isn't the slightest bit of fun. Why do we put ourselves through so much frustration and disappointment? I have felt the despair and disappointment that comes from feelings of helplessness myself on several occasions and wouldn't wish it on my worst enemy.

Though it seems we all experience feelings of helplessness at some stage, it never ceases to amaze me how human beings will fight through considerable discouragement and disappointment with the primary objective of overcoming the challenges in front of them. I have observed that those who quit early are in the minority. However, it does seem that the times we do experience despair and disappointment draw the majority of our attention. I believe we can all reach the highest levels of our potential and contribute to the greater good in significant ways.

Think about this for a minute. What if we knew exactly what we wanted to achieve, had a plan to achieve it, and never allowed any negative emotions or self-defeating thoughts to inhibit us, allowing us to execute what needs to be done to achieve our objectives? Do we believe we couldn't achieve our dreams? Do we think we couldn't make it happen?

When we learn how to cultivate a fearless mind, we can achieve whatever we set out to accomplish. A fearless mind is achieved when we have cleansed ourselves of the barriers that prevent us from reaching our greatest potential. We do this by learning to accept what we have control over and what we don't. Once we understand what is our responsibility and what isn't, then we are able to channel all our energy into mastering those aspects that we have direct responsibility for and not waste energy (emotional, mental, or physical) on those things that are not within our responsibility.

A great deal of energy is often wasted and directed toward aspects of our lives that are outside our direct control. The two most prominent areas of wasted energy are guilt and fear. Many individuals struggle with learning from the past and leaving it there. We all make mistakes and pretty much know it the moment we make them. If we are attentive to the moment, the lesson is learned. The error many people make is consistently allowing their attention to dwell on the mistakes of the past. When we allow our minds to dwell too much on the past, it impinges on our ability to live in the moment and enjoy the reality of what life has to offer. Why do we keep beating the horse? It is dead; move on.

A similar phenomenon occurs with fear. When we attend to what may or may not happen in the future, we open the door to fear. Our attention is again directed away from the moment, lowering our ability to make good decisions.

Say you are one of the tennis players on my team. You go out and play a match, giving it everything you've got, working hard to execute your plan, and maybe even diving for balls and scraping your knees. Having given everything you could, you come off the court with blood dripping from your knees and elbows. But you have lost.

How fair is it for me to rip you for losing the match? Do you have direct control over winning and losing? The opponent on the other side may have been older, wiser, bigger, or stronger. Maybe your opponent was from Australia, where they breed the athletes tougher (just kidding). If I were to hold you accountable for something you don't have direct control over, I would be setting you up for failure. Yet how many authority figures do this? How many parents do this to their children? How many coaches, teachers, and bosses do this? More important, how many of us do this to ourselves? We are setting ourselves up for failure when we expect outcomes that are not within our direct control. We are perpetuating failure in others when we treat others the same way.

How fun is it to work for a boss who evaluates our performance on variables we cannot control? Pay attention to coaches, bosses, or businesspersons that function in this way. I guarantee that they nearly always describe their employees as underachieving. Further, there is usually a high turnover of players or employees. Nobody wants to work or live in this type of environment. Finally, these authority figures themselves don't last long because their performance is greatly weakened by these poor thought processes.

Here is a good story to illustrate what I'm talking about. I have had the opportunity to coach many quality individuals through the years. I have worked with one individual since he was fifteen years old. He is now twenty-three and trying to make a go of the professional tennis tour. I have always respected this young man, as he has always been a class act. For years we worked on his game both mentally and physically, although I would have liked him to give more attention to the mental side of things. He ended up playing college tennis at the university where I coach the women's tennis team, so I was able to stay in close contact, meeting regularly with him to work on his mental performance.

With as close a relationship as I have had with this individual, I hope to one day turn on the TV and watch him win a big tennis tournament. There would be some pretty significant joy in seeing him reach his dreams and a sense of satisfaction that I contributed to his success to some degree. However, when the match is over, I will go back to my responsibilities and to my own life. I can't live his life, nor do I want to. I have to be responsible for those things over which I have direct control.

What we do with our allotted time here on this planet and what we make of our life is a direct reflection of the choices that we make. Our life-scripts and self-images are made up of daily decisions. These life-scripts that define our existence are written on our faces. When we look in a mirror, we see the life we've lived. What do you see? Lines of fulfillment, of a life well lived? Are you creating lines on your face that you want to see when you look in the mirror? Are you in control of your life?

I once heard a story about Abraham Lincoln that I cannot verify to be true, but I choose to believe it because it represents the kind of man I understand Abraham Lincoln to have been. On a specific occasion when President Lincoln was in his office, he was to meet with an individual. I have no knowledge of what the meeting was about, but as the story goes, the individual came into the president's office with such an attitude (portrayed by his body language and facial expressions) that President Lincoln sent the man out of the office without any discussion. President Lincoln's assistant, obviously surprised, inquired what the matter was; President Lincoln responded that he didn't like the expression on the man's face. He went on to explain that he believed we are responsible for the expressions we carry on our faces.

I have contemplated this story many times. It is meaningful to me because I believe we should be held accountable for those aspects of our lives over which we have control. It is empowering to take responsibility for those things that we can do something about. There are so many variables in this life that we can't control, it only seems logical to put all our resources into mastering those aspects of our lives that we can control.

To actually do this, to actually apply these principles, I require those with whom I work to use a structured Mental Skills Journal (a sample is shown on page 31) to help to channel their spiritual, emotional, mental, and physical energies. This journal gives individuals the opportunity to take responsibility for their lives and for their performances. It also supplements the need to develop our mental skills on a regular basis. We have a clear purpose and a strategic plan to achieve our purpose; then we provide feedback on the specifics of our performance. Growth is not only possible, it is inevitable. Even better, growth is accelerated, and we avoid the cycle of mediocrity. Since I began insisting that my clients use this journal, I have seen incredible spiritual, emotional, mental, and physical growth.

Note
1. Stephen Clissold, *St Teresa of Avila* (London: Sheldon Press, 1979), 150.

High Performance

"To laugh often and much; to win the respect of intelligent people and the affection of children; to earn the appreciation of honest critics and endure the betrayal of false friends; to appreciate beauty, to find the best in others; to leave the world a bit better, whether by a healthy child, a garden patch or a redeemed social condition; to know even one life has breathed easier because you have lived. This is to have succeeded."

—Ralph Waldo Emerson[1]

To me, high performance is not a phenomenon that just falls in our lap. It requires hard, smart work for years—sometimes even decades—before we can achieve it. Even then, high performance is not something that, once achieved, is ours forever. Ask those individuals who have achieved high performance, and they will tell you there really is no finish line. As soon as we achieve an objective, there is always another one to pursue.

High performers never really feel like they have arrived. There is always another level. To allow ourselves to believe we have arrived is a sure sign we have lost our focus. To high performers, it is about the journey. They understand that performance requires constant attention to the reality of the moment in order to achieve continual growth. We are not born great, and there are no fairy godmothers flying around sprinkling fairy dust on our heads and turning us into overnight superstars.

In order to reach our greatest potential, we need to stop fighting with ourselves and consolidate our energy for the purpose of achieving whatever it is we choose. British-based researchers Michael J. A. Howe,

Jane W. Davidson, and John A. Sloboda concluded in an extensive study that our innate physical skills are more of an indication of what we will not do rather than what we could become[2]—meaning, if we are short and skinny, becoming an offensive lineman on the football team is probably out of the question; if we are tall and heavy, gymnastics is probably not an option.

Nature, in some respects, points us in a general direction. When I was young, I played a lot of rugby. I loved it but decided to take a year off to focus on tennis. After the year off, I wanted to get back into rugby, but in that year I grew from medium height and build to tall and skinny. My mother, out of concern for my safety, would not let me play rugby again.

Inherent abilities can be a prerequisite to specific endeavors. From the choices that are left for us, genetics has little impact on how successful we could become. High performance is created. We have to want it; nobody can give it to us, and nobody can do it for us.

Let's take a closer look at what high performance is. Is it winning? Is it obtaining wealth? Is it power and influence? What does high performance mean to us? Think about that. To me high performance is being my very best. It brings peace and satisfaction. I don't have to be on a tennis court, in a boardroom, or in a classroom. And it is not only when things are going great in my life. It is any time or place when I am at my best.

High performance can be those moments when we're on a tennis court and everything is just rolling. We all have those days when we are performing some task so well that we feel we are inches away from perfection, when the hairs on the back of our neck stand up.

High performance also occurs when everything around us seems out of control, when people around us are losing control of their emotions, becoming irritated, frustrated, and angry, at times even with us. Despite all these outside challenges, we maintain control of our minds and, indirectly, our emotions. Maintaining focus on what needs to be done—increasing confidence and one's ability to make good decisions—results in high performance. High performance doesn't mean we have to be doing something great. Any task that is performed well is worthy of being called high performance.

At times, tremendous peace and satisfaction come when I am performing the simplest of tasks. The toughest task I have experienced to this point in my life is not staying in control during a championship match as a coach or a player, when my heart feels like it is located somewhere down in my stomach and I am doing everything I can to stay in control of my nerves; it is not staying in control when delivering my dissertation defense in front of professors ready to cut me to threads if I haven't done my homework with the utmost precision and accuracy. For me the toughest task I have experienced is staying in control when dealing with my four children—all eight years of age and under. I love them dearly, but when we are all tired, I face a great challenge. My wife performs this task every day with grace and self-control. I often wonder if underneath the water her feet are kicking like crazy. Above the surface she performs the role of parenting at far higher levels than I have been able to achieve, but I am working hard at it.

High performance is when those factors within our direct responsibility are being controlled and mastered—when we are completely at one with ourselves. These moments can be fleeting (they are for me, at least); but the more I experience them, the more precious they become. Every day I seek to perform better than the day before. It doesn't matter what the day holds for me; I just want to leave this mortal existence knowing I didn't waste a moment, that I gave my very best effort each and every day. To be at our best may seem a simple endeavor; to me there is a whole science behind the simple phrase "do your best."

Research supports the notion that high performance does not fall into anyone's lap. Success only comes through hard work over many years—and not just mindless hard work, but work that is precise and exact. There truly seems to be one narrow path to high performance but many paths to mediocrity. Professor K. Anders Ericsson of Florida State University explored the phenomenon of why, "in virtually every field of endeavor, most people learn quickly at first, then more slowly, and then stop developing completely."[3]

Ericsson and his colleagues concluded that "nobody is great without work."[4] This doesn't reveal much we didn't already know, but their study goes on to state that while hard work is critical, it isn't just any work—it is work of a particular kind. After all, many people work hard for years, even decades, without ever really improving, let alone accelerating their growth. These researchers called it "deliberate practice."[5] I personally like the phrase "paying attention to the details."

Note
1. Quoted in Anthony Robbins, *Unlimited Power* (New York: Fawcett Columbine, 1986), xxi.
2. Michael J. A. Howe, Jane W. Davidson, and John A. Sloboda, "Innate Talents: Reality of Myth?" *Behavioral and Brain Sciences* 21, no. 3 (1998): 339–442; cited in Geoffrey Colvin, "What It Takes To Be Great," *Fortune* 154, no. 9 (2006): 93.
3. Geoffrey Colvin, "What It Takes To Be Great," *Fortune* 154, no. 9 (2006): 93, summarizing K. Anders Ericsson, Ralf Th. Krampe, and Clemens Tesch-Römer, "The Role of Deliberate Practice in the Acquisition of Expert Performance," *Psychological Review* 100, no. 3 (1993): 363–406.
4. Geoffrey Colvin, "What It Takes To Be Great," *Fortune* 154, no. 9 (2006): 93.
5. K. Anders Ericsson, Ralf Th. Krampe, and Clemens Tesch-Römer, "The Role of Deliberate Practice in the Acquisition of Expert Performance," *Psychological Review* 100, no. 3 (1993): 367–68.

Deliberate Practice Defined

"The people who separate themselves in any line of work do so by being creative and by paying attention to detail. And neither of these things happen without energy and love. That's the secret to life."

—John Buccigross[1]

Deliberate practice is activity that does the following:

1. Is explicitly intended to improve performance
2. Reaches for objectives just beyond one's level of competence
3. Provides feedback on results
4. Involves high levels of repetition.[2]

TAKING A CLOSER LOOK AT THE definition of deliberate practice reveals an interesting concept. The first component of deliberate practice, "activity that's explicitly intended to improve performance," reinforces the mental need to focus attention on performance skills and not outcome skills—for example, "keeping the ball out in front on my ground strokes" in contrast to "I've got to win today." This shows how important it is to channel our mental energies toward objectives that we have direct control over, which in turn builds confidence and feelings of empowerment. In contrast, directing our mental energy toward objectives that we don't have direct control over greatly increases the level of anxiety and creating feelings of learned helplessness.

The second component of deliberate practice, "reaches for objectives just beyond one's level of competence," reinforces how important it is to have a clear objective to work toward. It provides

13

us with direction and helps motivate us toward a clear purpose. It is important to notice the specific details of this component of performance. It states that we need to be reaching, meaning we are always striving to get better, to grow.

The objective needs to be a little beyond reach so that we feel it is obtainable. If it is too far out of our reach or skill level, it only promotes thoughts and feelings of helplessness, prompting us to give up on our objectives or at least settle for less. This is why most New Year's resolutions fail. Last, if we don't continually set new objectives when an old one is obtained, we run the risk of complacency and further hinder development.

The third component of deliberate practice, "provides feedback on results," reinforces the importance of measuring performance in the development of skill and enhancing confidence. Providing feedback allows people to take responsibility for their own growth. Feedback is used to evaluate which skill sets are contributing to improved performance and what skill sets need to be isolated for continued improvement. For example, on many occasions when teaching private tennis lessons, I have worked with a student on a specific skill. By the end of the lesson, significant improvement in the skill is obvious, but at the next lesson the student more often than not is back to his or her old habits, doing what we had worked so hard to improve. I have wondered many times how many coaches are getting rich working with people that take no responsibility for their growth.

The last component of deliberate practice, "involves high levels of repetition," reinforces the importance of isolating skills and working on them over and over again until the skill is mastered. It is not just physical skills that need to be mastered; mental and emotional skills need honing as well. When we channel our energy in a deliberate way, it is possible to achieve almost anything. We see amazing feats of human achievement around us every day.

Here is an application of deliberate practice, for example: Simply hitting a bucket of tennis balls with no objective in mind is not deliberate practice—which is why most tennis players don't get better. Hitting twenty slice serves with the objective of placing the ball within two feet of the target 80 percent of the time, continually observing results and making appropriate adjustments, and doing that daily— that's deliberate practice.

Here is a story to illustrate the importance of and benefits that come from deliberate practice or paying attention to the details. Upon the completion of my thesis study, I was in the weight room one day talking with BYU's head strength and conditioning coach, Jay Omer. We got talking about the importance of paying attention to details. I relayed to him the findings of my study that showed that 76 percent of success at the collegiate level was attributed to commitment or self-motivation.

Coach Omer had just come to BYU from Georgia Tech (GT) and told me of a football player who had just been drafted from GT in the top ten, yet he had walked onto the team four years earlier. Coach Omer went on to explain that this athlete was extremely committed, worked hard, and paid close attention to all the little things in conditioning.

Coach Omer talked about how after the draft had come and gone, this athlete came to say his good-byes. Coach Omer had gone through his files on this athlete and noticed that in the four years he had been there, he had never missed a day of conditioning. The athlete turned to Coach Omer and said, "No, coach, I haven't missed a rep in four years."

I think that each day, we all do something pretty amazing, but we don't notice it and all too often direct our attention to the things that we didn't do well. The structured Mental Skills Journal that I require my clients to use forces them to write down three things they did well in short, concise detail. By doing this, they are attending to the details of their accomplishments. Hence, skill development is enhanced and a sense of fearlessness is developed.

Notes

1. John Buccigross, "Breaking down the Eastern Conference," espn.go.com, September 29, 2009 (accessed October 15, 2009).
2. Geoffrey Colvin, "What It Takes To Be Great," *Fortune* 154, no. 9 (2006): 94, summarizing K. Anders Ericsson, Ralf Th. Krampe, and Clemens Tesch-Römer, "The Role of Deliberate Practice in the Acquisition of Expert Performance," *Psychological Review* 100, no. 3 (1993): 367–68.

Four Components of Our Composition

"It's all about balance."

—Tiger Woods[1]

"It always comes down to how well you know yourself."

—Tiger Woods[2]

THERE ARE FOUR COMPONENTS OF OUR composition: spiritual, emotional, mental, and physical. The spiritual side is what gives us our direction and guidance on our journey through life. It is often manifest through our conscience. Some choose not to listen to their spiritual side and hence don't develop a deep sense of trust and confidence in themselves, often resulting in living a purposeless, aimless, meaningless life. Others choose to develop the skills necessary to listen to their spiritual side and find great confidence and comfort, giving them a real sense of purpose throughout their journey, a critical component to developing a fearless mind.

A good analogy for the spiritual side of our composition is driving a car. Those who know their destination and have mapped out the route they want to take get in a car and head toward their destination with a clear purpose and specific direction. Those who don't have a clear destination or have failed to plot their course end up driving around in circles. Many clients I have worked with have struggled to find meaning or purpose in their lives. They have no clear destination, and they find themselves spinning in circles, beating themselves up. Once a clear objective is determined, the negative, self-destructive

17

cycle is quickly broken, and the result is lowered anxiety, greater focus, confidence, and better decision making.

Here's an example. I had an amazing tennis player on my team. This young lady was not religious, so her purpose in life came through her tennis. She had been playing from a young age, always working toward achieving one level of performance and then moving on to the next level. Life was pretty simple, and she never really seemed to have any significant difficulties dealing with life's challenges.

She reached a very high level of athletic performance on the tennis court, even playing professionally after finishing her eligibility in college. However, eight months after finishing her tennis career, she fell into a destructive cycle. Because she was very passionate and driven, when she didn't have a clear purpose toward which to channel her energy (no objective), that energy was inadvertently channeled inward. She became moody and irritable, and she withdrew from her normal daily activities.

It got to the point where she didn't want to get out of bed in the morning. After coming to me for advice, I guided her back to using her Mental Skills Journal that she had used for many years for tennis. This time we came up with new objectives that were unrelated to tennis that channeled her energy toward becoming a better person instead of a better tennis player. She was already a great human being, but the pursuit of perfection is eternal. As soon as this individual had something to work toward on a daily basis, she almost instantly came out of her depressive state and was back to her usual happy self.

It is a simple concept. If we don't have a direction to channel our energy toward, it is easy to focus too much on what is wrong—what is wrong with ourselves or what is wrong with the world. This type of thinking can be very debilitating; this cycle is hard to break if an individual is unaware of the underlying cause. There are those that get stuck in this cycle and never really break free of it. When we do have something to focus on, our energy is channeled into motivating us to action. This falls in nicely with the next part of our composition.

The emotional side consists of our passions and desires that give us the energy to go after our objectives. Emotions are a good thing. We need emotions. If we didn't have any emotions, we would flatline, with no personality and no desire to do anything. A life without emotions is hard to contemplate. Would we even get out of bed in the morning if we didn't have emotions?

When our emotions are channeled in constructive ways, we become formidable at achieving whatever skill sets we focus on. Controlling emotions provides an individual with the ability to think rationally and reasonably, increasing the ability to learn from life events and perpetuate growth; hence, emotional energy is needed to get things done. However, when there is an overabundance of emotional energy, it can cause destructive behavior as well.

When we lose control of our emotions, we aren't thinking anymore; we are worrying. When we worry, our minds race, attending to events that occurred in the past and then jumping to events that might occur in the future. When we allow our minds to do this, we unwittingly perpetuate feelings of guilt and fear that inhibit our thought processes and restrict our decision making abilities. Guilt and fear don't exist in reality; they are created in our minds and exist in the abstract.

When we worry, our minds are not paying attention to the reality of the moment, and making good decisions can be very difficult, since important information is not being recognized and considered within our thought processes. When we are in the present, important information is recognized and processed—we call this thinking. Controlling our emotions perpetuates thinking and lessens worrying.

Here is an example of how not controlling our emotions may play out. Say an individual makes a mental mistake—as we all do every day at some point. It's not a big deal the majority of the time. However, many of us become irritated by our mistakes and let our emotions spiral out of control, allowing that irritation to turn into frustration or even anger.

Once we are in the anger stage of a self-destructive cycle, we are more likely to make numerous mistakes, compounding the mental mistake and digging a hole for ourselves that didn't have to be anywhere near as deep as it is. I like the example from the movie *The Hulk*. When Dr. Bruce Banner allows his heart rate to get over 200 beats per minute, he turns into the Hulk, a creature that has no control over himself and basically destroys everything within his reach. In contrast, when some people who have control over their emotions start to feel irritation or frustration, they channel that emotional energy into more productive avenues, like focusing on what they need to do at that moment or what they can do better the next time. They don't allow their emotions to turn molehills into mountains.

It is through our minds, the mental component, that we direct and coordinate the other three components of our composition. Our minds direct our attention to the spiritual promptings that guide us through our lives or direct our attention away from spiritual promptings. Also, it is our minds that direct our emotional energy into either constructive or destructive paths. Finally, it is our minds that command the physical side when we actually act. The mind is the driver, strategically planning what route we take to achieve our destination, choosing where to direct our emotional energy, and commanding the body to change gears, brake, accelerate, and so forth.

The mind, or more specifically, how we think, is not set in stone. We don't come out of the womb with the same thought patterns as we have when we are fifty years old. Just as it takes hard work and a lot of practice to develop the muscle memory to execute a certain skill, it takes hard work and a lot of practice to learn how to think in an effective, productive, fearless way.

Yet few people put any time into developing their thought processes. Many of us go to school to learn a skill or a trade, but what about learning to think the right way? Does this not come first? What's the point in learning a skill if we don't have control over our minds? I see this in athletes. They have amazing physical abilities that have been refined over years and years of sweat-inducing training, but they haven't developed their minds. Think about how our bodies would look if we never exercised. In contrast, look at what highly trained bodies can do. By spending time working on our thought processes, we can develop powerful tools and relish the challenges of life.

Some may believe that the physical component is the most important since in the end it is our works—our actions—that define who we are. But there is only one physical phenomenon that we experience that isn't first directed from the mind, and that is our reflexes. When our reflexes are at work, our senses react to stimuli in the environment and send a message to the central nervous system, which sends a message straight back to the body to act accordingly. This is the only time that the message doesn't go all the way to the mind, which is why we call these reactions reflexes. The average reflex action is 20–30 milliseconds for someone in their early to mid-twenties.

Reaction time is different from reflexes. When our senses pick up something in the environment, the message goes all the way to the brain, we make a decision, and the brain sends a message back to our muscles. The average reaction time for someone in their early to mid-twenties is 200 milliseconds. The fastest ever officially recorded reaction time was Babe Ruth at 120 milliseconds.[3] Simply put, the physical side does what the mind tells it to do. The more consistent and efficient our commands are, the swifter and more automatically the physical side reacts to mental commands.

In all my years of watching and studying why people do the things that they do, it has become very apparent to me that high-performing individuals think along very similar lines. Although I don't believe anyone could ever say that two people think exactly alike, nor would I ever propose that such a thing would be good, it does appear to me that there really is only one road to high performance but many roads to mediocrity.

When our minds are in tune with our spiritual side, channeling our emotions in constructive ways and efficiently communicating with our physical body, it feels like we are moving like a well-tuned engine. When this state of being is achieved, we put ourselves in a position to reach our greatest potential. Motivation is high, anxiety is low, concentration is enhanced, confidence is heightened, and decision making is improved.

Notes

1. Alex Tresniowski, *Tiger Virtues: 18 Proven Principles for Winning at Golf and in Life* (Philadelphia: Running Press, 2005), 166.
2. Ibid., 27.
3. Dr. Barry Schultz, University of Utah, Exercise Science Department, motor learning class, 2005.

Mediocrity

"Excuses and alibis prevent us from being accountable, for taking responsibility. Sure, it's part of our nature to blame others, but if you keep going down that road there can be no destination. Just road."

—Wayne Bennett[1]

ONE OF MY GREAT CONCERNS IS why so many individuals are getting lost in the murky waters of despair and discouragement. The rock group Nickelback said it best in their song "Rockstar": "It's like the bottom of the ninth and I'm never gonna win. This life hasn't turned out quite the way I want it to be."[2] I believe too many of us have felt this way too often.

Mediocrity is defined as "the quality or state of being mediocre."[3] Mediocre is defined as "of only moderate quality; not very good."[4] Is this what we all dream of, to be "not very good"? I have asked this question many times in my seminars, and I have yet to have anyone positively respond to this question, even in jest.

Mediocrity is the modern-day plague that affects many of us. Behavioral researchers tell us that as much as 77 percent of everything we think is negative and counterproductive. Medical researchers have found that as much as 75 percent of all illnesses are self-induced.[5] Further, research is inherently conservative in order to offset chance being an unforeseen predictor in the cause-and-effect relationship—meaning that, in reality, the numbers are probably even higher. Seeing such high percentages of the population battling self-defeating behaviors is a major concern.

What happened to our dreams and aspirations? More important, do dreams ever really come true? Researchers have concluded in an extensive study that "the evidence [they] have surveyed . . . does not support [the notion that] excelling is a consequence of possessing innate gifts."[6] That means reaching our truest potential and achieving our dreams is not beyond our powers of control. The researchers found that "a few do improve for years and even decades, and go on to greatness."[7] Why don't more of us reach our true potential? When we are young and innocent, anything and everything seems possible. We dream of being great athletes, or great singers, or a successful businessperson, or raising great children with patience and kindness. Do dreams become a reality, or are they just thoughts and images that exist only in the movies?

It has been my observation that people don't really give their dreams a chance. People talk about doing this or that, but few ever give it a go. I have seen very few people give the slightest effort to make their dreams a reality. Others try half-heartedly, giving inconsequential effort before bagging it for safer, more convenient endeavors. However, research tells us that the few who do give it a go become high performers through perseverance over long periods of time.[8] They maintain their focus on their objectives, set performance objectives they have direct control over, and evaluate their performance regularly—and ultimately make their dreams reality.

I believe the big question is, why do so many of us fall into this cycle of mediocrity? Why do so many of us settle for average behavior? Fear is definitely a component. It seems that a large majority of us settle because we are afraid of what the future holds. One subtle choice here or there can lead us down a path we never planned on taking. Unwittingly developing a fearful mind, we settle for what is safe and easy instead of pursuing our dreams.

My mother, second in generosity only to my wife, wanted me to get my undergraduate degree in accounting when I came to the United States to study and play tennis. My father was an accountant and owned his own accounting firm back home in Australia. My well-meaning mother wanted me to get a degree in accounting and go back and work with my dad when I graduated. This would have guaranteed financial security and a nice, safe life.

Just one problem: I didn't love accounting. It's not as if I hated it. But it was not my calling in life, that's for sure. I felt like I was selling myself out when I headed toward that objective for the first year and a half of undergraduate school. I still remember the day I switched to psychology. The day I switched majors, I was already into the second week of the semester and was sitting in an economics class, bored out of my mind.

I remember looking out the window at the Kimball Tower, which housed the psychology department, thinking I had to at least give my dream a chance, despite what my mother wanted. I remember waiting impatiently for the class to end so I could add Psychology 111 and drop my economics class. That first psychology class was the worst grade I got in college (brute of a teacher), but what mattered the most was I loved it.

Although I was afraid to change the direction I was heading (the accounting path was a safe, easy path), fear wasn't the only thing holding me back; it was more complex than that. It was the uncertainty and confusion within myself. At the time I wasn't sure if sports psychology was really my dream. Now, with three degrees in psychology and years of experience, I can look back on those times in my life with more clarity. I realize now that at the time my four composition components (spiritual, emotional, mental, and physical) didn't mesh. I was fighting myself, which created uncertainty and, ultimately, fear.

Notes

1. Wayne Bennett, *Don't Die with the Music in You* (Sydney: ABC Books, 2002), 84.
2. Nickelback, "Rockstar," *All the Right Reasons* (2005).
3. *The New Oxford American Dictionary*, s.v. "Mediocrity."
4. Ibid., s.v. "Mediocre."
5. Shad Helmstetter, *What to Say When You Talk to Yourself* (New York: Pocket Books, 1982), 21.
6. Michael J. A. Howe, Jane W. Davidson, and John A. Sloboda, "Innate Talents: Reality of Myth?" *Behavioral and Brain Sciences* 21, no. 3 (1998): 407, cited in Geoffrey Colvin, "What It Takes To Be Great," *Fortune* 154, no. 9 (2006): 93.
7. Geoffrey Colvin, "What It Takes To Be Great," Fortune 154, no. 9 (2006): 93.
8. Michael J. A. Howe, Jane W. Davidson, and John A. Sloboda, "Innate Talents: Reality of Myth?" *Behavioral and Brain Sciences* 21, no. 3 (1998): 404–6.

Midlife Crisis Phenomenon

*"Ninety-nine percent of failures come from people who
have the habit of making excuses."*
—George Washington Carver[1]

LET'S TAKE A CLOSE LOOK AT the phenomenon known as a "midlife crisis." A midlife crisis typically affects one's life in one's forties or fifties, but it can occur at any time when we lose perspective and purpose in our life. To understand what causes a midlife crisis, we need to bring our attention back to the beginning. As young children, we start out with dreams and aspirations. We spend our days playing, pretending to be Michael Jordan, Tiger Woods, Julia Roberts, Oprah Winfrey, Warren Buffet, or other successful people.

As we get older, our interests shift toward specific areas of greatest interest and enjoyment. We usually enjoy specific activities because we feel competent at them. Basically, we do things that we are good at. If we feel competent at a specific endeavor, it is highly likely that we will then spend more time participating in it. This results in greater growth of the specific skill sets needed to perform specified skills while simultaneously building self-confidence.

As our skill sets continue to grow, enjoyment continues to build. Eventually we hit a fork in the road and must make a choice: are we prepared to commit to do the things necessary to take whatever activities of interest we are engaged in to the next level? Taking it to the next level means putting our developed skill sets on the line for everyone to see and criticize. The next level takes great strength of character and of mind.

At this point our attention often switches from playing, having fun, and just trying to get better to focusing on winning. When we start to focus on winning, we open the door to worrying about losing. This switch of attention is an orientation issue and can occur at varying times in our lives. When it happens, our motivation switches from a process, task-oriented nature to an outcome, ego-oriented nature. The main point I want to bring up here is that when we are motivated by outcome objectives (winning), we are setting objectives over which we don't have direct control.

Therefore, an increase in perceived failures occurs, leading to less time and effort participating in the particular sport, resulting in slower skill development. The number of perceived failures it takes to result in reduced commitment and effort varies with each individual. With less commitment and effort, growth is hindered and individuals become more susceptible to settling for less than what they had originally dreamed.

Many endeavors lose participants through the years as individuals lose sight of their dreams because they feel at some point like they have failed to some degree or another. When I first started playing tennis, many men participated in tournaments. As the years went by, the draws got smaller and smaller—this occurrence was even more significant on the women's side than the men's. Because of perceived failures, over time, more and more people give up. When I first got into squad training (an invitation is required) when I was about fourteen, there was a group of roughly fifteen guys about my age. By the time I was seventeen, there was only one other guy from the original group that was still playing hard and chasing his dream.

This example reflects many endeavors from school, work, and life in general. Instead of studying a subject of interest, we often choose a subject to study that is convenient and safe, rather than trusting ourselves and choosing to stick with what we love. Too often we give in to self-doubt and allow fear to dictate our choices. Over time we give up on our dreams; we allow our minds to head down the path of fearful living instead of taking the road to fearless living.

Once we allow self-doubt to dominate our mindset, it is easy to lose sight of our dreams. As we leave the university, we often have a degree in something other than what we really wanted. From there we go into a job or career that we really didn't plan to work in. One subtle choice after another, we settle for less than our very best or for something other than what we truly love. As time moves on, we continue to do what comes next; years, even decades, pass by as we live our lives in reaction to life's challenges, playing the game of life to not lose.

We spend our days fulfilling what others want from us. We pay bills to fulfill someone else's objective to get money from us, instead of creating, doing, and controlling what we can control. Before we know it, we have been in our jobs or careers for fifteen to twenty years.

Then one day something jolts our memories back to when we dreamed of a different life, of a different career. All of a sudden a surge of repressed feelings of regret and unfulfillment comes flooding through us. We perceive our lives to be less than what we had once dreamed. We perceive that we haven't lived up to our fullest potential, that perhaps we are working a dead-end job, possibly have gained a few pounds, and maybe haven't been the good parents we had wanted to be.

So what do we do at the pinnacle of a midlife crisis? We go buy a Porsche—or at least that is what I would do—maybe a boat, a Harley-Davidson, or all of the above. Some grow a beard and go riding their hogs across the country with their buddies. Others do something more dramatic, like selling their homes and moving to another state or even another country.

The point is that the symptoms of a midlife crisis are attempts to take back something that has been perceived as lost. Repressed feelings from not chasing dreams can come in the form of buying a sports car or growing a beard. Not everyone goes through a midlife crisis, and its effects are different for everyone, some more severe than others.

Once the midlife crisis has run its course—when we stop feeling sorry for ourselves and stop attempting to fill a void—we realize we have responsibilities. Hopefully, we can refocus our mindset, take a positive look at our lives, and get busy doing what we can to live the life that we choose and not live someone else's idea of what our lives should be.

It is my belief that the midlife crisis can be avoided if we learn to develop and cultivate a fearless mind. When we are truly free to think for ourselves without the inhibiting effects of self-doubt and push ourselves to have the courage to stay focused on our objectives, the midlife crisis phenomenon can be avoided. On a side note, I believe it is important to realize as we move toward our objectives that other opportunities may come up that possibly fit our inner wishes more fully—we need to have the courage to adjust our objectives.

The important thing to remember is that when and if we tweak our life plan, we need to do it because we feel good about it, not in reaction to demands from others. I am not talking about the need to take a job because we need to pay bills; taking a job to satisfy needs is not settling for less. But putting a half-hearted effort into our job or quitting on long-term objectives and not looking to progress is settling for less.

To illustrate my point, when I was young I wanted to be a professional tennis player, but I was also very interested in why people do the things they do. My objective was to make a living as a professional tennis player. My friend and I planned on making it on the tour, buying a house in Germany, purchasing fast cars, and driving as fast as we could on the autobahns. I always wanted a Porsche 911. I continued down this path throughout my teenage years, turning pro at seventeen after finishing year twelve. However, at the age of sixteen I went to see a sports psychologist to figure out how I could do a better job of not beating up myself mentally.

I still remember that day like it was yesterday. The sports psychologist's name was Dr. Jeff Bond, and he worked at the Australian Institute of Sport. From the moment I met with Dr. Bond, I became fascinated with sports psychology. Afterward I would often wonder what it would be like to be a sports psychologist. I loved all sports, not just tennis. I also loved trying to understand the mind. (By the way, Dr. Bond diagnosed me as a perfectionist at the time and told me that I overanalyze.) Although I still wanted to be a professional tennis player, as time moved on I spent more of my time pondering the mental side of my tennis and life in general.

By the time my experience on the tour was over and I was on my way to the States to study and play collegiate tennis, my objective had changed to becoming a sports psychologist. My point is, don't get too locked into thinking that dreams won't ever change. They may. For some people they change regularly—a little too regularly. For others they change infrequently. I believe that many people find their calling in life only when they are actively chasing what they thought or hoped was their calling, only to discover their true purpose somewhere else.

For others, their job is just that: a job, not a career. But they still haven't settled for mediocrity because to them high performance isn't about what job they have; it is about how they perform their job. High performance has very little to do with the arena and an awful lot to do with mastering skills.

Becoming Fearless—At the end of each section I will illustrate how to apply the principles taught from the section in a text box like this one. The how-to applications of developing a fearless mind refer to the Mental Skills Journal, the greatest tool I have employed as an athlete, coach, and sports psychology consultant.

Sample Page from the Mental Skills Journal

1. Objective:
   Coach, Speak, TRAIN Internationally

2. Plan:
   Look for opportunities Internationally

3. Strengths:
   a. *Likability, NLP, 16,000 Coaching Calls +*
   b. *Skilled Coach + Speaker 100's of Conf Calls*
   c. *In the right Company 100's of TRAINING*

4. Weakness:
   a. _____

5. Performance:

Motivation	1	2	3	4	⑤
Anxiety	1	②	3	4	5
Concentration	1	2	3	④	5
Belief	1	2	3	4	⑤
Decision making	1	2	3	④	5

Note

1. WorldofQuotes.com: Historic Quotes and Proverbs Archive, Worldofquotes.com/author/George-Washington-Carver (accessed October 14, 2009).

Step I

MOTIVATION

A Good Start

"When a winner fails, he trains harder while a loser blames others."
—Wayne Bennett[1]

To ILLUSTRATE THE SIGNIFICANCE OF BEING motivated by appropriate objectives, here is a real-life example of how two individuals with similar objectives achieved completely different careers—mainly due to contrasting mindsets. One experienced a fairly average tennis career (myself), and the other progressed rapidly enough to eventually become the number-one tennis player in the world.

When I was twelve years old, a group of fifteen guys trained in my uncle's squad. We were the best players in the state, for the most part. Of this group, not everyone wanted to become a professional tennis player, but I would say the majority had dreams of winning Wimbledon someday. We all worked hard, but some worked harder than others.

A few years later, only two of us from that original group were still spending significant time on tennis. By age sixteen, my friend and I had moved into a group formed from a larger population base. These guys were from states across the country and were all motivated like my friend and I to make it on the professional tennis tour. We trained in our respective states but often traveled together to tournaments, stayed at each other's houses, and practiced together.

Of the ten or twelve in this group, some were very talented, some less talented; some were hard working, and others not so hard working. I thought several of them would make it on the professional tour. I hoped that if I worked hard enough and could keep up with them, maybe someday my perseverance would pay off. At the same time, I didn't feel like I was the worst of the group.

Of those I thought had the best chance to make it, one of them made it for a while before injuries derailed his career. I lost track of another guy I thought was extremely talented, but I did hear he lost his passion for the game. The most successful one among us was at the time the weakest in our group. He was a year younger, and there was nothing special about his physical game that I can remember.

What stands out in my memory is that he had the greatest weapon anyone could have: his mind was wired the right way, or rather he was programming his mind the right way to maximize and accelerate his growth. He had a fearless mind. Having a fearless mind enabled him to develop his skill sets more rapidly than the rest of us. This mindset allowed him to be in the moment and learn from his experiences the first or second time around, unlike the majority of us who need ten to twenty experiences to learn a lesson.

His name is Patrick Rafter, and he was number one in the world for a while; he won the U.S. Open twice—no small feat. Before I left for the States to accept a tennis scholarship, and while he was preparing for the Australian Open, I played him in a best-of-five-set practice match, which he won 7–6, 7–6, 7–6. I could see that he had developed a fearless mind, and I had to work to keep up with him. The physical differences weren't that dramatic, but Patrick Rafter became number one in the world—and that started with the wild card he drew for the Australian Open where he started to make his presence known.

Six years later, Patrick won his second U.S. Open title, enjoying his time atop the world rankings. I, on the other hand, was finishing a pretty ordinary college career. The difference in the paths that Patrick and I took is, I believe, due largely to the differences in our motivational orientations.

Why do some make it and others don't? This question has puzzled me for many years. At the time of the practice match with Pat, I thought it was largely out of my control. I believed that some had it and others didn't. Now, after years of playing, coaching, and studying the mind, I see how Pat's mental skill sets were far superior to my own (and to most of those guys' who I grew up competing against). The mental skills that Pat possessed can be learned; we just need to know what they are and how to learn them. The mental skills identified in this book represent the types of skill sets Pat exhibited when we played. It is my opinion that these skills were the determining factor in his successful climb up the professional tennis rankings.

Note
1. Wayne Bennett, *Don't Die with the Music in You* (Sydney: ABC Books, 2002), 62.

Task vs. Ego Orientation

*"It is possible to fail in many ways . . .
while to succeed is possible only in one way."*

—Aristotle[1]

BEHAVIOR IS SAID TO BE ROOTED in one of two forms: task or ego. A task is defined as "a piece of work to be done or undertaken."[2] Hence, task-oriented individuals are focused on what needs to be done. Ego is defined as "a person's sense of self-esteem or self-importance."[3] Ego-oriented individuals are focused on how outcomes affect their self-worth.

Research has shown that task-oriented individuals persist at tasks longer, choose more challenging tasks, work harder, and perform better in testing environments (meaning they perform better under pressure). Ego-oriented individuals show less persistence, choose extreme objectives (either very easy or very hard), have a weaker work ethic, and don't perform as well in testing situations (meaning they don't handle high-pressure situations very well).[4]

Task-oriented behavior is also known as performance orientation. Performance-oriented objectives imply behaviors or actions that are directly related to the task at hand and not the individual. For example, they say, "I want to hit my forehand consistently crosscourt with good spin"; "I want to stay focused on what I want to do while under pressure"; "I want to catch anything that I get a finger on today"; "I want to jump seventeen feet today at the track meet."

Ego-oriented behavior is also known as outcome orientation. Outcome-oriented objectives imply attention directed toward the

39

result. For example, "I have to win today or else"; "I have to finish first this weekend"; "We are going to win the tournament this week, or else my coach isn't going to think much of me."

Task-oriented individuals have approach tendencies. They play to win; they play because competition is fun and enjoyable. They enjoy seeing what they can do under pressure. Task-oriented individuals seem to stay very focused on the present; hence, they experience fewer signs of fear. Tiger Woods once said, "Whatever is in the past has already been done. I'm trying to do the best I can in the here and now, and if I started thinking about what I've done in the past, I'll forget about hitting a nice, high, shaping 2-iron up there."[5]

Ego-oriented individuals have avoidance tendencies. They play to avoid embarrassment—meaning they play not to lose. They are often preoccupied with the future and with what others may think of them. They act like the weight of the world is on their shoulders. They play like they have everything to lose and nothing to gain.

Are we born with certain tendencies? Can we do anything about what motivates us? In fact, our orientations are conditioned in us through our environment. Although there are exceptions, our primary motivation is those things that have been communicated to us the most often. For example, if we are told repeatedly as a child, "Do your best, that is all that matters," chances are we will be primarily motivated by task-oriented objectives. On the other hand, if we have been told most of our lives to win at all costs, we are more likely to be motivated by ego-oriented objectives.

Can our orientation change? Yes. Can we be motivated by both orientations at the same time or even at different stages? Yes. Is it even possible to be motivated by both orientations from one moment to the next? Absolutely. What motivates us can and does change from one moment to the next. Let me give you an example of how quickly our mindset can switch from task orientation to ego orientation.

One of my freshman tennis players (we will call her Rita) played against a freshman on Notre Dame's team. Rita was a very good junior player, but the player from Notre Dame achieved higher levels of performance. The girl from Notre Dame had a significant edge in her confidence, based on previous performance accomplishments (the number-one factor in building confidence). At the beginning of the match, Rita was executing her game plan with authority and without hesitation. She was not thinking about the score, just the task at hand. Rita got ahead 5–2, then realized the gravity of the situation, and her body language completely changed. I could tell Rita was thinking about winning the set, maybe even about winning the match.

Rita immediately got caught late, the physiological symptom of high anxiety (Hick's law tells us the more we think, the slower we react). I encouraged her to focus on the task and to tell herself she could do it. Her opponent sensed the hesitation and picked up her game. From this point on, it was a battle for Rita to get her anxiety under control so she could perform as she had earlier. She lost the next five games and the first set. Rita fought hard in the second set but was not able to change the momentum, losing the match in straight sets.

This example shows how quickly focus can shift from task-oriented to ego-oriented. It takes time to develop good mental habits so our thoughts don't betray us at critical moments, or at least to know how to deal with unwanted thoughts that pop into our minds and not allow single thoughts to explode into crippling self-doubt.

Just as it takes hours, days, and even years to perfect a forehand, it takes hours, days, and even years to learn to control our minds. At high levels of performance, one wrong thought can be very costly. That's why it is so much fun: the challenge of performing a task so well we don't know how we could do it better, the joy in testing our limits. This is why we push ourselves toward perfection.

I remember loving to hit the ball when I first started playing tennis, but more than anything I loved trying to master the skill sets required of the sport. I got addicted to tennis while I was still playing baseball and football (rugby league). I loved game days for both baseball and football, but practices were boring. Tennis was fun every day, whether it was a match or just practice. I loved seeing my progress every time I stepped on the court. There were so many skill sets to master. It got to the point where I had to play every day of the week. As the years rolled by, I realized I wasn't so much addicted to tennis as I was addicted to self-mastery. I loved seeing how good I could get performing each stroke.

Notes
1.   David Ross, trans., *The Nicomachean Ethics of Aristotle* (London: Oxford University Press, 1961), 38.
2.   *The New Oxford American Dictionary*, s.v. "Task."

3. Ibid., s.v. "Ego."

4. Craig Manning, "Attentional Control across Performance Levels in Tennis Players" (PhD dissertation, University of Utah, 2007), 45–46.

5. Alex Tresniowski, *Tiger Virtues: 18 Proven Principles for Winning at Golf and in Life*, (Philadelphia: Running Press, 2005), 46.

Stages of Development

"If you want to be mentally tough, . . .
follow your beliefs and don't give in to yourself."
—Steve Waugh[1]

THERE IS A PATTERN TO MOST people's lives in how they develop their respective frames of mind. Ericsson and colleagues found that the large majority of the human population tends to go through three stages of development, while a few take paths less traveled.[2]

During the first stage of development, growth is rapid. Attention is on improvement, not on winning or outcome objectives. We exhibit high levels of motivation at this stage because growth is fun. When we are young, before we become corrupted by the cares of the world, we "play," messing around with friends and playing sports. The more we play, the more our skill sets are developed. One's self-worth is not on the line; therefore motivation and enjoyment are high. As we progress and mature in our measured society, we feel compelled to engage in activities where there are winners and losers. These opportunities shift attention to more outcome-oriented ways of thinking. Playing for fun and getting better begin to take a back seat.

During the second stage of development, growth slows down. Attention shifts toward winning and losing (outcome objectives), and since we don't have direct control over winning, anxiety is heightened. In addition, winning is abnormal. For example, in the most recent Australian Open tennis tournament, in the men's singles draw alone, there were 256 entrants, including qualifiers and main-draw participants. If we define ourselves on outcome objectives, there were

255 losers and only one winner. When we don't win as often as we would like, or rather when we don't perceive the results in a positive light, it is easy to get discouraged over time and apply less effort.

During the third stage of development, growth is stopped completely. At this stage individuals become so frustrated with their perceived lack of success that they quit. This quitting isn't usually a dramatic event, although it can be. It usually takes the form of subtle choices and actions to not pursue dreams anymore. At times we may continue on the same path we have been on—not wanting to admit to others or even ourselves that we have lost hope, going through the motions without our original enthusiasm and commitment.

I know this stage well; I lived through it. Once I finished high school and went pro, I realized it was not for me. I was living in a different hotel every week, sleeping on the floor, worrying about every penny I was spending. I didn't like the lifestyle at all. More important, I didn't like how selfish I became.

When we have a desire to be a pro athlete, it can become a very self-centered pursuit. Although I realize now it doesn't have to be that way, at the time I thought the only way to get out of the negative cycle I was in was to quit playing on the tour. This was difficult because I had spent so much of my time and resources, and my parents' time and money, to become a pro player. I continued masquerading on the tour for a year and a half while trying to figure out what I really wanted to do with my life.

It was a very hard time. Looking back, I realize that it is vitally important for us to always be working toward something, to have a clear purpose; otherwise we can get stuck swimming around in circles and fighting with ourselves. Knowing where we are heading allows us to channel our energy toward a clear objective. Further, when we don't have a clear objective, we become more susceptible to self-defeating behaviors. There is so much static that surrounds us in our everyday lives. It is easy to get depressed if we allow our mental energies to be directed in ways that are not in our best interest.

I was traveling the world playing tennis, but I was far from happy. I view those eighteen months as the worst time in my life. My mental energy was being channeled against myself instead of for myself. Our late teenage years to early twenties are supposed to be great years. They weren't for me. I have spent my life since then attempting to help people to be happier, healthier individuals equipped with fearless minds so they can live more productive lives. To many, this may not seem an exciting life, but to me, it is my calling in life.

When I realized the pro tour wasn't for me, I found it very hard to focus on what I was doing. I pushed myself physically to the point that I almost threw up in practice. I didn't realize it at the time, but now I can see with more clarity and realize that I had given up mentally. I overcompensated physically in an attempt to hide my mental shortcomings. It all came to a head at a local tennis tournament over the Christmas holidays back in Australia. With my parents in attendance, I had a minor mental breakdown while playing a semi-final match against a guy I had always beaten easily in the past.

It was a small tournament an hour and a half from my home. I had been on the tour for eighteen months, so I should have been winning easily. But I had just lost the second set and had to play a third set. I was so focused on the outcome, on winning, that my anxiety was incredibly high. I was the ultimate perfectionist, always wanting to please my parents, coaches, and friends. This was the first set I had lost the whole tournament, but after losing the set I went crazy, yelling, smacking balls around, subconsciously hoping someone would save me from myself.

I think the umpire was too afraid to give me a point penalty. My mother had never seen me behave like this. I always held everything in, attempting to show a brave face to the external world. I ended up winning the third set easily because I was so mad at myself, but the damage had been done. I didn't like who I was becoming. After the match my parents and I went to get something to eat, and I found the nerve to tell them I didn't want to play tennis anymore. I apologized for wasting their time and money and being so selfish all those years. They never questioned my decision. I guess they could see the pain and anguish I was suffering, but I couldn't bring myself to use the word *quit*. I had to tell myself I was retiring; the word *quit* felt wrong. In reality, I had quit a year earlier. I had been living a lie.

This is a dramatic example of what can happen to us during the third stage of development if we don't follow our dreams and approach our objectives appropriately: burn-out at the age of twenty. It shouldn't happen, but it does every day, in all walks of life. It all starts with the goals that we set. If we get off on the wrong path at the beginning, all sorts of things can go wrong; but if we start on the right path, many other problems fall away or never appear.

"The correct path": that's what I call it. The researchers that coined the developmental stages didn't give this stage a name. I can't call it the fourth stage of development because it is a divergent path. It doesn't follow from the third stage in any way. If I had to say when this stage starts, I would say it begins somewhere after the first stage and before the second stage.

This stage of development, or the correct path, is rooted in what researchers contend is where only a few of us "improve for years even decades, and go on to greatness."[3] It is the path chosen by those who stay focused on task-oriented objectives and who never become corrupted by the expectations and static surrounding them. This path has no finish line. The focus is on the journey, on perpetually learning from each situation. The mind is fearless, freeing the individual's potential. Thus our growth is accelerated at a far greater rate than that of the average fellow, resulting in objectives being achieved more consistently, further perpetuating rapid growth and even the attainment of higher objectives.

The correct path isn't contingent just upon hard work for years or even decades. After all, as Geoffrey Colvin points out in a *Fortune* article about deliberate practice research, "Many people work hard for decades without approaching greatness or even significantly getting better."[4] When an individual follows the principles of deliberate practice, tasks or skill sets are enhanced. The attentional demand required to execute deliberate practice is very much in the present. When individuals discipline their minds to attend to the present, feelings of control are enhanced. It is when minds are allowed to jump from the past to the future, without much attention to the present, that feelings of uncertainty persist. Further, individuals that discipline their minds to attend to the present have greater capacity to adapt to real situations, allowing ~~for optimal~~ decision making and ultimately greater execution of strategies.

Finally, when individuals feel they have more control over their current situations, they generate feelings of empowerment, develop greater confidence, and enhance enjoyment of performing tasks the best they can (the joy of self-mastery, of self-growth is a major component of the fearless mind).

In contrast, ego-oriented behavior attributes success and failure to self-worth. When ego-oriented individuals win, they think more of themselves; when they lose, they think less of themselves. Self-worth becomes very fragile and is dependent on outcome when the outcome is often not within the direct control of the individual. Therefore, one's self-worth is contingent on variables outside of one's immediate control, resulting in a significant rise in anxiety. Simply put, ego-oriented individuals put their happiness in the hands of others, resulting in unstable frames of mind and up-and-down performances.

Notes

1. Steve Waugh, foreword in Wayne Bennett, *Don't Die with the Music in You* (Sydney: ABC Books, 2002), 21.
2. K. Anders Ericsson, "The Influence of Experience and Deliberate Practice on the Development of Superior Expert Performance," in *The Cambridge Handbook of Expertise and Expert Performance*, edited by K. Anders Ericsson, Neil Charness, Robert R. Hoffman, and Paul J. Feltovich (New York: Cambridge University Press, 2006), 685.
3. Geoffrey Colvin, "What It Takes To Be Great," *Fortune* 154, no. 9 (2006): 93.
4. Ibid., 93–94.

Perfectionism

"Someone once asked me, 'Why do you always insist on taking the hard road?' and I replied, 'Why do you assume I see two roads?"
—**Author unknown**

THE PERFECTIONISM STATE OF MIND IS the most common psychological issue that I deal with as a sports psychology consultant. In today's high-pressure world, the expectation to perform multiple tasks at the same time with increasingly higher levels of efficiency is causing more and more individuals to suffer psychological breakdowns. Having been diagnosed as a perfectionist myself, perfectionism is something I know well. I have studied, pondered, experimented, and practiced varying approaches on how best to overcome what can become a very debilitating state of mind if left untouched.

Throughout my younger years, I repeatedly engaged in self-defeating thoughts. This was never more evident than when I was on the tennis court. I would get down on myself whenever the outcome didn't go as I wanted. I obviously had the objective of winning, but whenever I played football or baseball, I never seemed to struggle with self-pity; I never wanted to let the team down. I remember one incident on the football field. I played five-eight for our rugby team, which is the pivot position—in other words, I was the one directing the plays.

I had our backs lined out about to go on the offense deep in our opponent's territory. I was yelling at them to spread out and be ready, and as the half-back passed me the ball, I took my eyes off it and dropped it. When I turned around, the guys on the team had their heads down, mad at me. Instead of feeling sorry for myself, I started yelling at them to get back on defense.

I never felt sorry for myself when I played team sports. But this was not the case when I played tennis. Because I had no one else on the court with me, it seemed a lot easier to get down on myself whenever I didn't win. When I look back on my younger tennis playing days, I can almost feel the self-pity, the head dropping experiences. Tennis or any sport is a microcosm of life: the best and worst of ourselves are magnified for everyone to see, including ourselves. I have learned things about myself on the tennis court I am still not sure I ever needed to know, but I have become stronger and, in the end, happier for the tough times I have been through dealing with perfectionism, self-pity, and ego-oriented behavior.

After arriving in the United States, my coach at the time—because of my self-destructive behavior on the court—told me to go see a sports psychologist to help me stop getting so down on myself. At the time we didn't have sports psychologists employed at BYU, so I went to a general psychologist on campus. I will never forget this experience because it helped redirect my career path.

Upon meeting with this particular psychologist, I told him what had been going on with me in my life and in particular on the tennis court. After listening to what I had to say, the psychologist went on to diagnose me as a perfectionist. He explained that because I was always setting objectives that were too high, I would inevitably fall short, feel sorry for myself for a period of time, get ticked off, and then set even higher objectives, and the cycle would repeat. Over and over again I would do this to myself. Obviously, I never felt like I accomplished anything. It is almost impossible for anyone to keep their heads up and not feel sorry for themselves when they repeatedly feel like they are falling short. It is hard to deal with feelings of inadequacy on a daily basis. Nothing ever feels good enough.

I said, "Yeah, you got it, that is exactly what I do." I remember feeling this massive sense of relief that someone knew what I was going through. I felt a glimmer of hope that maybe I wasn't destined for failure. And then nothing. . . . I kept looking at the psychologist, waiting for him to say something. It felt like an eternity, and that wave of relief I had felt suddenly turned into a sense of dread as it became obvious that this guy didn't know what I needed to do to overcome this perfectionist characteristic I had struggled with for so long.

I sat there waiting for him to say something. He had diagnosed me well, but as every second passed, the tension increased. It couldn't have been more than ten seconds, but to someone who felt like he was carrying the weight of the world on his shoulders, ten seconds was an eternity. He finally spoke, asking another question: "You are probably always on time?"

"Yes," I replied, not sure where this was going.

He then told me he wanted me to show up fifteen minutes late to my next appointment because I needed to learn to relax. I didn't mean to be disrespectful, because I appreciated the information he gave me, but this guy's lack of understanding as to how to apply—how to do something about my situation—ticked me off. I have since found that this occurs a lot in life. People are good at talking and expressing what's wrong with this or that but have little capacity to do anything about it. I decided right then that I was going to figure out a way to help people like myself do something about their struggles and not just diagnose their problems.

I left wondering how being late on purpose would help me to relax more. I went ahead and set my appointment in my planner for a quarter past the hour (fifteen minutes after the normal appointment time). As you would expect from a perfectionist, I turned up right on time— fifteen minutes late—or was I on time? I never could decide which was which. Needless to say, I decided to study perfectionism myself. Here are my conclusions from that research and from my battles with perfectionism.

First, many people are not egomaniacs but exhibit similar behavior patterns as those motivated by their egos. These individuals are passionate, caring, hardworking individuals who are always trying to please others. They struggle with outcome-oriented behavior, meaning they set objectives that are always in the future.

As we have already learned, when we set outcome objectives, high anxiety is often the result. To apply these principles to real-life situations I will use a tennis player as an example. But it could be any athlete, businessman, homemaker, or other person. Life is performance. We are all performing every day. A task-oriented tennis player is likely to set an objective such as, "I want to stay focused on one point at a time; I want to hit my ground strokes deep with consistency—say

4–8 balls each point—and finally, I want to get in tight on the net."
As we can see, nothing has been said about winning or losing. These
objectives are all task-oriented skill sets. Whether mental or physical
in nature, it doesn't matter.

When we direct our attention to isolated tasks and evaluate
our efforts on a consistent basis, improvement is achieved—often at
accelerated rates. The result or outcome (wins and losses) is a by-
product of the performance. If we perform well (execute those skill sets
to our maximum potential), the chances of winning greatly increase.

Further, as we can see from these objectives, they are all within
direct control of the individual. This creates an environment that
dramatically increases the chances of success. In addition, skill level
and confidence are reinforced at increased rates due to feelings of
empowerment that are generated when we feel like we have control.
When we set expectations that are within our direct control, it is
possible to always have a good experience, to feel worthwhile instead
of helpless. Some may say that this just sugarcoats things, but it is
quite the opposite. Setting task-oriented objectives provides a mental
framework where we are held accountable for what we have control
over.

When one of my players doesn't achieve specific minimum levels of
performance, consequences follow. As a coach, how fair would it be for
me to hold my players accountable for winning a match when they are
playing someone older, wiser, and more talented? Do they have direct
control over winning the match? This approach only increases feelings
of helplessness. Holding an individual accountable for task objectives
that I have set in partnership with the individual is logically fair.

The only way we cannot achieve objectives that are within our direct
control is when we engage in self-defeating behavior. When a coach
sugarcoats self-defeating behavior, it only perpetuates the behavior.
When we engage in self-defeating behaviors, we prevent growth—or
at least accelerated growth—and slow the development to the point
that dreams are not achieved; hence, mediocrity is reinforced.

When we are accountable for our own lives, growth is inevitable.
It is just a matter of time before our objectives are achieved. Finally,
performers (again, we are all performing every day, no matter what we
do) who set task objectives find that there is much more to life than
just winning and losing. They become open to all the intricacies of life.

Paying attention to the details of performance allows growth to be maximized while increasing the quality of what we do.

In contrast, an ego-oriented individual is likely to set an objective such as, "I have to win today." An objective like this creates high levels of anxiety because an individual doesn't have direct control over winning and losing a tennis match. I could play the best match of my life, diving for balls, scraping my knees, leaving blood on the court, and hitting my serve harder than I have ever hit it; but if my opponent is simply a better, older, wiser tennis player, the objective is often unobtainable. When we constantly direct our attention to the future, we open the door to fear.

Fear

"I never think of the future. It comes soon enough."
　　—Albert Einstein[1]

WHAT IS FEAR? CAN YOU SHOW me fear? It's not possible, is it? We can only show the symptoms of fear; we cannot show fear itself. Fear doesn't exist in reality. It lives in our minds, in the abstract. I remember a class I was taking for my PhD. The professor had organized the class so that we were all sitting in a circle. He went around the circle, asking each of us what we were afraid of. By the time he got to me, I couldn't think of anything, so I said crocodiles.

I am from Australia, and crocodiles are aggressive creatures. They will take us even when they are not hungry. I heard a story about a man who was dangling his legs off the edge of a wharf when a croc grabbed him and took him into the death roll. As the man was taken into the water, he hit his head on the wharf and it knocked him out. Because his body was limp, the croc must have assumed he was dead and put him on a ledge for later. Luckily the guy woke up and swam to safety.

My professor laughed at my example of what I was afraid of and used my fear of crocodiles as the example to explain fear. He asked me to visualize being in a room with no way out except for one door. He then said to visualize a croc coming around the corner. In the moment the croc came around the corner, what would I likely be thinking about? My response was, "I would be afraid of being bitten and how badly it was going to hurt. The pain, I guess, is what I would be afraid of, and the damage it could do to my body." My mentor went on to explain that all these thoughts lie in the future. Fear only exists in our thoughts of what may or may not happen in the future. He then asked, "And what would you be thinking if the croc was actually biting your leg?" My response was that I would be punching, kicking, and fighting it.

"Exactly," he said. "You would be dealing with the situation and there would be no time for fear." He went on to explain that in the moment, there is only action. If you were being attacked, you would be directing your attention to the task at hand and just dealing with it. When we allow our minds to worry about the future, we open the door to fear. Paulo Coelho said, "If you pay attention to the present, you can improve upon it. And, if you improve on the present, what comes later will also be better."[2] We attend to the present in the hope that whatever we improve upon in the here and now will benefit us down the road.

Fear can have a major impact on our lives through the objectives that we set. Actually, setting objectives has been found to be the single greatest cause behind psychological issues in human achievement. Yet haven't we always been told to set goals (objectives)? Setting a clear objective is important; the challenge is in setting objectives that we have control over, or rather over which we perceive we have control. Ericsson, who authored the landmark research on deliberate practice back in 1993, says that objectives should be just a little beyond our reach.[3] When we set objectives that are too far out, it is too easy to get discouraged and give up on them.

This is why people struggle with New Year's resolutions. People start with good intentions, but because their objectives are disproportionate to their current situations, they inevitably set themselves up to fail. I see this happen repeatedly in all walks of life. When we set objectives too far beyond our reach, we allow variables that we don't have direct control over to impact our journey toward our objectives. Ultimately this results in perceived failures, and eventually people quit trying.

It is very disconcerting to see so many individuals settling for less than their best. Life is difficult enough without setting ourselves up to fail. Unfortunately, I have witnessed this over and over again with clients.

A football player who was struggling terribly with perfectionist characteristics came to me for help. After meeting with him, it was apparent he was trying to please everyone around him. He was completely motivated by outcome objectives and trying to keep everyone in his life happy; but this group of people didn't just include his parents and siblings. He wanted to please his coaches, his teammates, and all the folks from his hometown. He was the town's pride and joy.

This young man was so overwhelmed with the pressure he was feeling that he started suffering from migraine headaches, which caused him to miss a lot of class time; hence, he was failing several of his classes. His anxiety was so severe that his hair started to fall out. I worked with this young man for only a couple of weeks to help him restructure his objectives in life, basically reprogramming his mind to attend to more appropriate stimuli.

This entailed getting him to search deep inside to decide what he wanted from life—not what his parents, siblings, the town folks, or anyone else wanted, but what he wanted—giving him a clear objective or purpose for why he was here. Then we focused on realistic skill sets he had direct control over that would lead to his objective. These objectives were always just a little beyond his reach—motivating him, but not discouraging him.

Once he achieved one objective, we had another already in place. He would celebrate achieving the objective but would then move on to the next. We also went through in detail those skill sets or tasks that he would need to master to achieve his objectives. These tasks were always within his direct control, consistently setting him up to succeed.

For two weeks we worked to restructure how he approached life. After two weeks he came by and said, "I am doing great. I don't need you." I was a little shocked and concerned because it usually takes a little longer to break a habit, and I didn't want this young man to relapse into old habits. He promised me he would continue to use the Mental Skills Journal.

I saw him about six months later. At first glance I noticed that his hair had grown back and his body language seemed to express a lightness that had not existed when I first met him. He told me he was engaged, school was going as well as could be expected, and football was going great. I knew football was going well—he had started every game that year on a very tough BYU team.

It definitely doesn't always happen this fast, but setting clear objectives is of the utmost importance. When we set appropriate objectives, fear has very little, if any, room to exist in our daily mental processing. When we set inappropriate objectives, we open the door to fear. In some cases we are not just opening the door, but inviting bad mental habits to come live with us. Taking this analogy further, some of us even feed bad habits, inviting them to stay for long periods of time.

Setting the right objectives helps us get where we want to be—it is that simple. Set the wrong objectives, and we swim around and around in circles of mediocrity. I am not saying that we all need objectives of supremacy to feel successful and worthwhile; if that is your purpose in life, then set a plan and go do it. What I am saying is that we all can be higher performing, no matter what we do in life, if we develop more of a fearless mindset. I do believe we all come prewired with a need to feel like we are contributing to society in some way to feel useful. If we are motivated in the right way, we can always feel useful and can accomplish our objectives.

Notes

1. Elizabeth Knowles, ed., *The Oxford Dictionary of Quotations*, 6th ed. (New York: Oxford, 2004), s.v. "Einstein, Albert."
2. Paulo Coelho, *The Alchemist* (New York: HarperCollins, 1998), 103.
3. K. Anders Ericsson, "The Influence of Experience and Deliberate Practice on the Development of Superior Expert Performance," in *The Cambridge Handbook of Expertise and Expert Performance*, edited by K. Anders Ericsson, Neil Charness, Robert R. Hoffman, and Paul J. Feltovich (New York: Cambridge University Press, 2006), 701.

Performance Mindset Scale

"We are what we repeatedly do. Excellence, then, is not an act but a habit."

—Will Durant[1]

IN MY EXPERIENCE, UNDERSTANDING THE DIFFERENT mindsets that motivate us can help us understand what we are trying to do. Here is my interpretation of varying mindsets.

> *Arrogance* is an "I'm good, you stink" approach.
> *Cockiness* is an "I'm good and I'm telling everyone" approach.
> *Confidence* is an "I am good" approach.
> *Passiveness* is an "I am not very good" approach.
> *Pessimism* is a "You are good, I stink" approach.

Arrogance and pessimism are two mindsets that I feel are not conducive to high performance (or even mediocre performance, for that matter). Both mental processes involve comparison with another. Therefore, one's state of mind is dependent on the performance of others. I don't recommend anyone ever evaluate his or her own life in comparison to another's; when doing this we put our happiness in the hands of others.

Cockiness is next on my mental attributes scale. It is not my chosen course of behavior, but I have never been bothered by it or seen any real problem with it. The main reason for this is there is no comparison with others. As long as another is not being put down or made to feel inferior, then I don't have a problem. Who cares if they need to tell people how good they are? Who is that hurting?

Confidence is obviously the best approach to high performance. I don't believe there is any limit to how much confidence one can have. Actually, I believe we need to store as much confidence away as possible.

Just to clarify, arrogance and confidence are two separate entities. There is no comparison with others with confidence. Arrogance is dependent on the comparison with others. Confident individuals don't care what anyone else is doing; they are responsible for what they are doing. The competition is with oneself, the battle of self-mastery. Arrogant individuals mistakenly believe that being better than someone else actually makes them good. But what if those being held in comparison actually aren't that good in the first place?

I have seen too many athletes think they are doing well when they beat a certain individual, when in reality both performances were well below what could be perceived as good. Remember this: being better than someone else may not make us good, just bad instead of very bad. Regarding pessimism, there is only one person who can stop us from obtaining our dreams, and that is ourself. There simply is no time for self-pity.

Note
1. Will Durant, *The Story of Philosophy: The Lives and Opinions of the Great Philosophers of the Western World* (New York: Simon & Schuster Paperbacks, 2005), 61.

Stories of Motivation

"Only those who dare to fail greatly can ever achieve greatly."
—Robert F. Kennedy[1]

LET ME ILLUSTRATE HOW BEING MOTIVATED the right way can be the difference between mediocrity and high performance. The decision whether to give a full athletic scholarship to an athlete is a big one. At y university a full scholarship amounts to approximately $70,000 over the four years. This doesn't include all the expenses incurred from training, traveling, equipment, and so forth, and it doesn't include a possible fifth year, which has become almost the norm these days.

Once we have decided that a certain athlete is the right fit for our program, then comes the tricky part: persuading the athlete to come play at our university instead of one of the other 314 women's tennis programs across the country. A bad decision usually means four years of carrying a player that never contributes to our program while getting a free education and countless hours of free coaching, nutrition, sports psychology, conditioning, and more.

With eight full scholarships to offer per NCAA regulations for women's tennis, and needing six players to field a lineup, we can sometimes absorb one less-than-wonderful choice; but if we make two poor choices, our program is highly likely to struggle for a period of time. Once our program is deemed to be headed in the wrong direction, it takes an act on par with parting the Red Sea to turn things around. Four years of not meeting athletic administrators' expectations is just enough time to lose our employment in this "win or else" era in which we live.

Is college recruiting a scary, nerve-rattling, do-or-die, luck-driven event where we let the dice roll and pray that we are having a good day? Or is it an enjoyable, exhilarating, challenging experience that tests one's ability to interpret hidden talents and weigh the many variables that impact the potential growth of fellow human beings who want so desperately to belong, to feel worthwhile and useful in this crazy world? Obviously the answer depends largely on what motivates us. It is the objectives and expectations that we place on ourselves that determine our perspectives and define who we are and what we do.

Here is a story that illustrates how being motivated the right way can have a tremendous impact on your life. I still remember the day like it was yesterday. My assistant and I were standing on an adjacent court in the indoor tennis facility at BYU watching two new players. It was early January, the first day of practice, a week and a half before our first match of the season. The two newest players on our team were hitting with each other. We had brought them in midyear, hoping they would bolster the program.

At first observation, it was apparent that one of the two young women was significantly more physically gifted than the other. I will call her Hailey. Hailey was muscular, medium height, had a strong body, was blessed with fast-twitch muscle fiber (coaching talk for someone who is explosive), had free-flowing strokes, and apparently had been well coached, with modern-day, heavy topspin ground strokes. She had great serve and volley skills and a serious no-nonsense approach to her tennis.

The other athlete was tall and lanky, with no muscle definition whatsoever on her legs, and had not been blessed with fast-twitch muscle fiber. I will call her Olivia. Her strokes were ten, maybe twenty years out of date. She did not hit the ball with the slightest bit of spin. About thirty minutes into the practice, I asked my assistant what her thoughts were on the two new players. Her response reflected my own: "Well, at least one of the two will be able to help us this year." She was referring to Hailey, the physically gifted one. It was one of those days that are bittersweet—feelings of comfort and relief that all our work may have paid off, but also feelings of disappointment that a mistake may have been made, at least from an athletic standpoint.

Four years later, both Hailey and Olivia were finishing up their senior years. Olivia, the less physically gifted athlete of the two, was finishing her tennis career as not only our number-one tennis player on a national, top twenty-five ranked team, but one of the players in BYU tennis history with the most wins. Olivia reached a ranking of sixteen in the country her senior year.

Despite our early observations about Olivia's lack of physical talent, she was very coachable. She did everything we asked her to do. But even more important, it seemed like we would teach her something once, and we wouldn't have to teach her that specific skill again. As coaches we were able to move forward onto other more advanced skill sets at an accelerated rate. Over time Olivia was able to take what physical skills she had and magnify her strengths, leveraging her potential to heights I never expected.

In her first year she played at the three and four positions for us, winning 50 percent of her matches. Her sophomore year she again played at the three and four positions, winning 73 percent of her matches. During her junior year, she played number two and won 82 percent of her matches (going 18–4), finishing with a national ranking of 99. Finally, during her senior year, she played number one, going 15–1 before developing a stress fracture in her foot. At the time she was ranked sixteenth in the country.

Instead of resting and letting her foot recover so she would be ready for individual nationals at the end of the year, Olivia chose to continue playing to help the team. Unfortunately, this resulted in her losing the final eight matches of her career and finishing twenty-fifth in the country. The consistent growth that is evidenced throughout Olivia's career shows what can be done with an individual who develops a fearless mind. She was, and still is, a great example of what can be done with the right mindset.

To illustrate the frailty and the importance of maintaining the correct mindset, here is another story involving Olivia during her senior year. At the beginning of her senior year she played pretty solidly, winning the BYU invitational. We then played a tournament in California. A player from Florida was the best player in the country at the time. I was very impressed with her mechanics, footwork, focus, and overall attitude. I told all my players to watch her body language and try to learn as much as they could from this individual. Modeling is one of the best ways to learn and grow. However, at the time I wasn't smart enough to think that maybe, at some point in the future, one of our players would go up against her.

Olivia watched this player a couple of times to learn what she could do to supplement her performance. At the time Olivia was ranked about eightieth in the country. Later in the fall we were playing in our regional tournament, and Olivia ended up pulling out a couple of tough matches and getting to the final. This was good enough for her to qualify for indoor nationals (the top thirty-two players in the country participate).

At indoor nationals, Olivia's first match was against a player that was ranked in the twenties, so a win over a player like this would be huge. Olivia got up 4–1 in the first set by focusing on her game plan and executing flawlessly. Then she allowed her mind to foster some doubts about whether she could keep playing at this level. She allowed herself to think that she wasn't supposed to be beating this player. In these moments she lost focus and couldn't concentrate on the cues that had allowed her to perform so well. Olivia ended up losing the next five games in a row to lose the first set 6–4.

She continued to play poorly in the second set, getting down 1–4, just two games from losing the match and finding herself out of the tournament and on a plane back to Utah. On the changeover at 1–4 down, I tried a different approach. Olivia was obviously overcome with fear and was uncharacteristically not responding to my suggestions on the previous changeovers due to the increased anxiety created from the magnitude of the event. In a last-ditch effort to get Olivia to refocus on the right things, I said to her as she sat down, "Hurry up and get this over with so we can go get a steak; I'm hungry."

She turned and glared at me. I figured being mad at me was better than feeling sorry for herself. I told her she wasn't playing her game, so what was the point in being out there? I asked her if she was having fun. She didn't answer, which was an answer in itself. I told her if she was too scared to play her game, then let's get it done and go find an Outback Steakhouse. She went back on the court, ticked off at me but more focused. Olivia started playing fearless tennis, got in a zone, and came back and won five games in a row to win the second set 6–4, just as her opponent had done to her in the first. She managed to maintain this mindset the rest of the match and closed out the third set 6–0.

As we left the courts, I went to check the draw to see what time she was scheduled to play the next day. I like taking matches and life in general one challenge at a time. As I looked at the draw, I noticed she was to play the player from Florida that I had built up on two previous occasions. I felt like an idiot. As we went out to the car, Olivia asked me what time she played and I told her. She then asked what was wrong. I couldn't believe what I had done, and now I wasn't controlling my emotions well on top of it.

I explained what was on my mind and apologized. Olivia, being the person she was, didn't seem to let it affect her. We talked over dinner about what she had done well that day, reinforcing the positives and addressing one aspect of her performance that she would like to do better the next day. The following day Olivia came out and played great tennis in the first set, the best tennis I had ever seen from her. She still lost the set 6–4, but it was fun-to-watch, high-level tennis.

On the changeover following the first set, Olivia sat down quite frustrated. I asked what she thought about the match to this point. She responded with, "I am doing everything I am supposed to do. What is wrong?" Even the best of us are a little emotional in the heat of battle. I didn't respond the best way. I chuckled a little, which just made her madder. I then responded with, "You are playing great—better tennis than yesterday. This player you are playing should be on the pro tour." This didn't go over well either. She gave me the same glare that I had received the day before. I hadn't seen this glare until this tournament, but, then again, I had never really used reverse psychology of this magnitude with her before, either.

I refocused and told her, "You are doing everything great; you just need to do everything faster, quicker. Don't change your strategy one bit, just execute better." She went out on the court and moved faster, reacted quicker. The ball was going back and forth so quickly (the ultimate sign of high-level tennis) that I found myself sitting there just enjoying the quality of tennis, lost in the moments as they passed by. Before I knew it, Olivia was up 5–2, 40–15 in the second set. To this day, it was the best college tennis I have seen.

The points were so fast, everything was happening so quickly, that I can see why people pay money to watch people perform at high levels. Her mind was so attuned to what she was doing that she seemed completely in the moment and absolutely fearless. At double set point, Olivia hit a serve that pulled her opponent off the court, and the player hit a weak return that looked like it wouldn't clear the net. After hitting the return, realizing the weakness of her shot, she hit the ground with her racket and stood in the same spot, apparently giving up on the point. Olivia stepped up to the weak return and hit what looked like a winner down the line.

Unfortunately, the ball clipped the tape and bounced high in the air. The girl decided to run for the ball. Here was Olivia, standing at the net watching this girl run from one side of the court to the other. Olivia was standing at the net helpless. The girl got to the ball and hit one of the ugliest shots I have seen. I don't think the ball ever came into contact with the strings; it pretty much was all racket frame.

In the end, Olivia could not get to the ball as it limped past her, barely out of reach. I didn't think much of it at the time; Olivia still had another set point, and her opponent appeared to be on the verge of completely coming apart. On the second set point Olivia missed the first serve and then . . . missed the second, double fault. I could see the anxiety all over her face, and it was very unusual for Olivia to show so much emotion. In that moment I knew she was in trouble. Next point . . . she double-faulted again. And then . . . again, three double faults in a row to lose the game.

The player from Florida settled down, realizing Olivia was imploding, and started to control her game again. The following game Olivia did not make a return. Four first serves, four returns into the net. On the changeover at 5–4 up, Olivia was visibly distraught. She was making comments like, "I hate this, I can't stand tennis, I don't know why I am even here." It is interesting how fast we can go from total control to total chaos. I tried to help Olivia refocus on what she needed to do. She started to play better, but by this time momentum had swung completely back in favor of her opponent from Florida. The girl came back and won the second set and the match 7–6.

It was interesting to see how fragile our focus can be—how we can be so focused on the right things one moment and completely lose it the next. It takes work to get in the right mindset, but it takes work to maintain it as well. I wouldn't say it is hard to achieve and maintain a fearless mind, but it does require constant attention to the reality of the moment.

What impressed me the most was after the match, with everyone leaving and the club organizers starting to turn off the lights, Olivia sat on the bench next to me and asked, "What do I need to do to get better?" Her comment took me by surprise. Here was a young woman that had come from nowhere as a freshman to become one of the top players in college tennis. She had just finished a fall semester where she had played the best tennis of her life.

She only had one semester of college tennis left, and she still wanted to find a way to get better. To those of you reading this, you are probably thinking, "Why is he so excited that she wanted to get better?" It is because once we have learned and have a deep understanding that high performance is about continual growth, the greatest battle has been won. I have worked with many athletes as a tennis coach and sports psychology consultant, and this is the number-one reason many get stuck in cycles of mediocrity. It takes a mammoth effort to get individuals to attend to growth and not be consumed with winning.

I reviewed with Olivia what she had done well, reinforcing the positives as always, and got her to pick just one thing she felt she needed to improve. After we were done, we went and got that steak, medium rare with vegetables. We hadn't gotten one the night before; since Olivia had won her match, we ate pasta instead. Steak is typically an after-match meal, not a pre-match meal. Now that the tournament was over, it was time for that steak.

Becoming Fearless—In order to motivate ourselves in such a way that inspires us to action, it is important to set objectives that are just outside our reach—thereby stimulating effort in the pursuit of the objective. The first step in the Mental Skills Journal is to set an objective for the day that channels your energy in a productive way. Writing down your objective each day commits you to a purpose. It is easy to fall off the path to high performance if you do not know where you are going. Also, it is helpful to remind yourselves why you are doing what you are doing. If I were a sprinter in track, my objective would be the next most reasonable time from my personal best time. For example, if my personal best was 11.4, my objective would be 11.2. An 11.2 time does not seem that far away, thereby motivating me to work harder and smarter. Once I achieved the time of 11.2, I would then adjust my objective to 11.0. If I were to set my objective too far away, say from 11.4 to 10.0, it is highly likely I would feel overwhelmed and lose motivation.

Note

1. Robert F. Kennedy, *To Seek a Newer World* (Garden City, NY: Doubleday, 1967), 232.

Step 2

ANXIETY

Is Anxiety Good or Bad?

"[The average human] looks without seeing, listens without hearing, touches without feeling, eats without tasting, moves without physical awareness, inhales without awareness of odour or fragrance, and talks without thinking."

—Leonardo da Vinci[1]

ANXIETY IS DEFINED AS "A FEELING of worry, nervousness, or unease, typically about an imminent event or something with an uncertain outcome."[2] Interpretation: when we don't feel like we have control, anxiety increases significantly. When we do feel like we have control, anxiety decreases significantly.

Is anxiety bad? Although we tend to perceive anxiety as negative, it can be a normal "alarm system" alerting us to danger. At times it provides us with the energy to get things done. Here is a story to illustrate how anxiety is a necessary part of our existence and can be positive in our lives at times.

I have had the opportunity to take my family back to Australia on a couple of occasions. One particular trip seems to have been imprinted in my memory more than others. I needed to go down to Sydney to watch a couple of tennis players that some friends had told me about. They were apparently very talented but didn't have outstanding results—diamond-in-the-rough types. Hence, I needed to see them with my own eyes to make sure they were good enough.

I thought I would just nick down and back without much fuss, maybe meet my mum in Sydney to catch up. My wife, being the thoughtful person that she is, suggested that I take my two oldest children with me to see the family while down there. After the twenty-four hours

71

it takes to get down to Australia, we got up early to get a jump-start on what we needed to do. As we walked out of the hotel heading in a direction that required crossing a busy road, my daughter, Abby, who was six at the time and had a ton of energy, bolted off. Anxiety hit me that she wasn't looking in the right direction for the oncoming cars. As everyone knows, Australians drive on the correct side of the road, which just happens to be the left side.

I ran after her and grabbed her moments before she stepped out into oncoming traffic. My heart was pounding, and perspiration had already built up in that short burst. The anxiety provided me with the intense energy to do something.

Another situation occurred on the same trip. After getting all my work done in Sydney, I took the children down to Canberra to see the family. It was late spring, so the weather was quite warm. My mum lives on five acres about fifteen minutes out of Canberra, so there's a considerable amount of long grass. We were having dinner, and Abby was sitting across from me, facing the glass sliding doors that overlook the acreage.

I was about to bite into a delicious steak when my daughter yelled something unintelligible, jumped out of her seat, and bolted out the door. I was not as quick to react this time, since I did not immediately sense any danger. As I turned to see what she was so excited about, I noticed a kangaroo out in the field and Abby running after it with shorts on, and no shoes. My mum, in a bit of a panic, told me to go after her because there were snakes in the field.

Again, the anxiety rush hit me, and I jumped up and chased her. Of course the kangaroo bounded away as Abby got close, which only prompted her to continue running farther across the field. I reached her after she'd crossed the entire field. Needless to say, my anxiety did not come down as I carried Abby back to the house—I didn't have any shoes on, either. I remember like it was yesterday, telling myself over and over again, "Please, no snakes, please, no snakes." Anxiety is a normal component of our composition. We don't want to get rid of our anxiety, but we do need to learn to control it.

High anxiety for extended periods of time is not generally a good thing; often it gives us a sense of dread or fear for no apparent reason, or at least no logical reason. When I was young and preparing for a big tennis match and feeling quite uptight, an adult figure that I respected saw me sitting nervously in the clubhouse and came over to ask me, "Are you nervous?"

My response was, "Yes."

This individual followed up with, "Good, you are supposed to be."

Being the overanalyzer that I am, I took that to mean that being nervous was a normal part of the performance process, and there wasn't much I could or should do about it. Hence, I never tried to lower or control my anxiety in my junior days. This resulted in me tightening up under pressure situations and choking, which led to some ordinary performances.

When I look back now, I can make better sense of what was going through my mind during this situation. My mistake was taking the comment "You are supposed to be nervous" too literally. I have learned that anxiety is normal, but high anxiety is not often a good thing. Our minds, just like our bodies, typically overreact to foreign circumstances. When we sprain an ankle, the body overreacts, creating excessive swelling in the ankle area as the body attempts to protect itself. The problem is that in order to diagnose and treat the injury, we need to reduce the swelling. The natural overreaction of the body is not always a good thing.

The same is true for the mind. When we sense a psychological threat, our minds overreact just as the body does with a sprained ankle. The only difference is, instead of a swollen ankle, we get swollen anxiety. The swollen mind needs to be reduced so it, too, can function at its best. There is a time and place for anxiety, and we cannot, nor do we want to, get rid of anxiety altogether. However, we need to learn to control it, to channel it in more positive, productive ways.

By learning to control our thoughts, we prevent anxiety from disrupting our everyday lives. The root of so many problems in today's society is high anxiety; it is alarming how many people are at odds with themselves and don't have a clear understanding of their own identities. We see this everywhere we turn: at the grocery store where people are snapping at each other for taking longer than expected in line, or on the road where people are engaging in road rage, or in our schools, or in the workplace for that matter, where bullies dominate others in their attempt to feel more secure about themselves. Taking things to a more serious level, our suicide rates and drug use (both illegal and legal) are at all-time highs, largely the result of anxiety disrupting each individual's sense of well-being.

Symptoms of anxiety include the following: muscle tension, trembling, shortness of breath, fast heartbeat, dry mouth, dizziness, nausea, irritability, loss of sleep, and finally, not being able to concentrate. How does anxiety affect us? Our body mistakenly triggers our alarm system when there is no danger.

How do we control our anxiety? There are numerous simple ways of alleviating anxiety that are common knowledge. Learning to relax (muscle relaxation, yoga, or deep breathing); exercising regularly (exercise can give us a sense of well-being and help decrease feelings of anxiety); getting plenty of sleep; avoiding alcohol and drug abuse (it is false to think that alcohol and drugs relax us; in the long run they make anxiety worse and cause more problems); avoiding caffeine (caffeine can increase our anxiety because it stimulates the nervous system); and confronting our challenges (having a planned approach to how we are going to attack, visualizing the situation, and practicing our response).

We don't have to think too long or too hard to figure out how these various skills can impact our anxiety. These are pretty much common sense. The problem is, in our busy lives, we don't always have the time and resources to get the necessary sleep and exercise needed to significantly lower our anxiety. In some cases, the thought of trying to fit in a workout at the gym only increases anxiety.

There have been times in my life when I was been eating and sleeping appropriately and getting tons of exercise (training four hours a day), yet my anxiety was at such high levels that I was suffering from migraine headaches a couple of times a week. Don't get me wrong: eating, sleeping, and exercising appropriately are important to our general well-being. What I am saying is that at times it isn't enough. The most important way I have found to lower and control anxiety is through setting appropriate objectives and expectations.

It all starts with setting the right objective. The objectives we set motivate us. If we are not setting appropriate objectives and expectations for ourselves, it doesn't matter how much sleep or exercise we get or how good our eating habits are. Anxiety is affected more by our origin of motivation than anything else. Research tells us that task-oriented individuals typically have lower anxiety because they set expectations that are within their direct control.[3] When task-oriented individuals feel like they have control over their lives, they are likely to feel more secure about themselves. Feelings of empowerment and confidence are significantly enhanced, creating a fearless attitude of "Let's see what I can do," and "This is fun; I love the challenge."

Simply put, task-oriented individuals are focused on performing the task and thereby don't take things personally. They are less likely to feel threatened by anyone or anything. They play the game of life with fearlessness. Winning and losing are not direct reflections on who they are as human beings. Anxiety is never really an issue of their performances.

Research also tells us that ego-oriented individuals typically have higher anxiety.[4] Ego-oriented individuals usually set expectations that are not within their direct control; anxiety goes up dramatically. Feelings of helplessness are heightened, increasing their sense of insecurity about themselves and about their environment. This results in attitudes of "I have to beat this guy today," "If we don't win today, I will not be happy," "If I don't get straight A's like my sister, my parents won't think as much of me," and "I hope I don't mess up in front of everyone." Ego-oriented individuals are not as interested in the challenge of the game as in how they are going to look.

Ego-oriented individuals are often at war with themselves. Common phrases to describe the behavior pattern of an ego-oriented individual are "They are battling with themselves" or "They are dealing with their inner demons." The reason is caused by high levels of anxiety that they carry on their shoulders throughout their lives, burning excessive amounts of mental and emotional energy. When that energy is exhausted, breakdowns occur.

If we watch Roger Federer, Tom Brady, Tim Duncan, Lance Armstrong, or any clutch performer, we will notice that they perform at extremely high levels for extended periods of time because they are not wasting energy. Their mental approach to what they do doesn't vary significantly. In fact, we could take any high-performing athlete, business executive, doctor, lawyer, or anyone else who performs at a high level consistently and compare their mental approaches to what they do, and we would find similar cognitive patterns. Again, there is one path to high performance, but many paths to mediocrity.

Notes

1. As quoted in Michael J. Gelb, *How to Think Like Leonardo da Vinci: Seven Steps to Genius Every Day* (New York: Dell, 1998), 97.
2. *The New Oxford American Dictionary*, s.v. "Anxiety."
3. Craig Manning, "Attentional Control across Performance Levels in Tennis Players" (PhD dissertation, University of Utah, 2007), 46.
4. Ibid., 11, 46.

Overanalyzing

"The more things you think about, the slower you react."
—Hick's law[1]

EVER SINCE I HAVE BEEN WORKING as a sports psychology consultant, I have found an alarming number of individuals who are overanalyzers. Their minds are consumed with worrying and not thinking. Let me break this down in more detail. While at a recent tournament, I found myself pondering over why so many individuals perform so poorly under pressure. I understand that pressure is nearly always going to lower an individual's performance. Only a rare individual performs better in pressure situations than non-pressure situations. Often, these individuals are poor practice performers because of a lack of focus. If they put more focus into practices, they would have less anxiety during matches.

Performing at less than one's best under pressure seems to be largely due to overthinking, or in other words, worrying. I don't know how many times someone has said to me after I've given a less-than-stellar performance, "You think too much, you need to stop thinking and just play." Thanks, but how do I do that? How do I stop thinking? Doesn't consciousness imply thinking? If I were not thinking, then I would be unconscious, right? If I am unconscious, I would have to be either asleep or comatose. So the comment to stop thinking so much is foolish. Rather than "stop thinking," we need to learn how to channel our minds in such ways that they don't interfere with our performances.

This is how I define worrying and thinking. Worrying is allowing our minds to attend to the future (fear) and the past (guilt). Oftentimes the mind is jumping from the future to the past and back again, resulting in a chaotic, hyper, undisciplined mind. Thinking, on the other hand, is attending to the present, focusing on what needs to be done from one moment to the next, adjusting to the demands of the moment, heightening the learning process, and minimizing the anxiety that is often built up.

When a twenty-one-year-old baseball player was sent up from the minors to pitch for the first time in the major leagues, anyone would guess that he was probably nervous. However, in his first four starts he only surrendered two earned runs. Over the next five starts he had an ERA (earned runs against) of 13.06—not good. Later that year he talked about how he thought his struggles were a result of him overthinking and that he needed to think less.[2] Hick's law states that the more we think, the slower we react. I pose the question, is the issue that we need to think less, or do we need to worry less? A fearless mind incorporates thinking but not worrying.

When another young pitcher who had been given the tag of "the next great pitcher" was struggling with mediocrity, he lamented after several less-than-stellar performances, "I was just thinking too much."[3] He was overanalyzing and overthinking. Overanalyzing is worrying, and worrying is fraught with anxiety. When we suffer from high anxiety, we no longer feel our way through performances. Instead, we hesitate and second-guess ourselves, making life harder than it needs to be.

Yet another young projected superstar in the minor leagues found himself struggling after earning a promotion from single A to double A. Instead of staying focused on the task at hand, as he had done in single A, he allowed his mind to shift to a point of focus that was not advantageous to his growth. He said that instead of worrying (thinking) about how to deal with the advanced level of pitching, his mind was thinking (worrying) about how he could quickly get a contract to get to the major leagues.[4] What this athlete didn't realize is that opening the door to outcome thinking only allows anxiety to creep in, concentration to go out the window, confidence to take a hit, and decision making to drop off. Ultimately, his overall performance dropped off significantly.

Research has shown that high levels of anxiety can cause distraction, which leads to a failure to detect important cues in the environment.[5]

Translation: the mind is all over the place when anxiety gets too high, preventing one from paying attention to important aspects needed for performance. Errors of omission affect overall performance negatively. Research on arousal level (not to be mistaken for anxiety level) has shown that "as arousal heightens during competition, the attentional demands of the skill become increasingly difficult. When this occurs, [an athlete's] visual field narrows, eliminating essential cues for optimal attentional control, and performance is negatively affected."[6] In summary, high anxiety causes distractibility, and high arousal causes narrowing of vision. This means that if we don't focus on the right things, we are up a creek without a paddle.

I spent a lot of time and money on the pro tour my first year out of high school. In the first round of one of my first pro tournaments in Queensland, Australia, I played a guy whom I thought I could beat pretty comfortably (not the right way to think); but I lost badly. As I was walking off the court and heading toward the clubhouse, one of my friends came up to me and asked how the match went. I responded with "2 and 2" (tennis talk for 6–2, 6–2). He followed with congratulations. I interjected with a firm, "No, I lost." His response was not completely unexpected, but still, the look of disgust in his eyes only made me feel worse. My friend went on to ask, "Did you play his forehand?" My heart sank even deeper as I thought, "Could I have lost yet another match because I was so focused on my worries that I didn't notice a fatal flaw in my opponent's game that could have changed everything?"

My friend went on to explain how my opponent had a great backhand but a nonexistent forehand. I couldn't believe how big of a moron I could be. Now, when I look back with more clarity, I see how my high anxiety led me to focus on what I was doing wrong. I trained as hard or harder than anyone, but my growth was nonexistent because I was always attuned to what I did wrong and wasn't paying attention to the moment and what could be learned. I was preoccupied with my issues, with what was wrong with my backhand.

I cringe at the thought of how many tennis matches I have lost because I allowed my anxiety to reign unchecked. Even worse, how many times in my life have I made things worse or not recognized simple solutions to problems because my mind was so clouded with unreasonable, irrational thoughts? I wonder how often in my life I have missed important learning opportunities that could have accelerated my understanding of the world and helped me improve my quality of life. Paying excessive attention to what is wrong only magnifies the problems.

I have come to realize how important it is to discipline my mind—to pay attention to the moment and not worry about the past or the future, to really focus on what I am doing, not what I am doing wrong. When I do this, the quality of my life goes up considerably. Paying attention to important cues allows me to adjust my approach depending on what I perceive needs to be done better. I find I have more courage to do what the moment demands.

Notes

1. As summarized by Dr. Barry Schultz, University of Utah, motor learning class, 2005.
2. Mark Bowman, "Notes: Davies Determined to Deliver: Right-hander over His Struggles, Regaining Confidence," mlb.com, February 19, 2007 (accessed October 14, 2009).
3. Mark Bowman, "Lerew Impresses at Spring Training: Right-handed Prospect Went 7–9 with a 5.26 ERA in 2006," atlanta.braves. mlb.com, February 19, 2007 (accessed October 14, 2009).
4. Mark Bowman, "Saltalamacchia Takes New Approach: Catching Prospect Trying to Focus on Present, Not Future," mlb.com, February 26, 2007 (accessed October 14, 2009).
5. Craig Manning, "Attentional Control across Performance Levels in Tennis Players" (PhD dissertation, University of Utah, 2007), 48.
6. Ibid., 24.

The Law of Attraction

"Whether you think that you can or that you can't, you are usually right."

—Henry Ford[1]

SAY WE ARE ON A TEE at a golf course that has water to the left and fairway to the right. Visualize standing there with the club in your hands, looking down the fairway; you have practiced your swing a couple of times and are ready to hit your shot when the thought pops into your mind, *Don't hit it in the water.*

What happens every time we think this way and then we swing? We hit it in the water. The reason is, the mind is not a reality meter; it doesn't innately know right from wrong. It only knows right from wrong because of what we have told it is right and wrong. Just thinking about not doing something brings what we are thinking about front and center. Here is another example. Visualize the *Mona Lisa.* Once you have a clear image of what the *Mona Lisa* looks like in your head, continue reading. "Do not image the *Mona Lisa* with a mustache!" instructs Michael J. Gelb in *How to Think Like Leonardo da Vinci.*[2] What did you do? You thought of the *Mona Lisa* with a mustache, didn't you? Unless you weren't really paying attention to what you were reading, it is unavoidable.

These examples illustrate how quickly the mind turns thoughts into mental images. Telling ourselves to not do something at times is actually like programming ourselves to do it. This evidence further supports the idea of not worrying, but rather thinking about what we want to do. Instead of telling ourselves, "Don't hit the ball in the

81

water," we need to train ourselves to say, "I want to hit the ball over there (fairway)." After missing a first serve, we cannot say to ourselves, "Don't double-fault." We need to program our minds to say, "I want to hit the ball there" or "I am going to hit the ball there."

This way of thinking is very assertive, not passive or aggressive. This applies to everything we do in life. When we are tired and we keep telling ourselves, "I am so tired," what chance do we have of pulling out of our tiredness? Think about anything in life that we have told ourselves over and over again that we would not or could not do. What has happened in all of those situations?

My poor control over anxiety caused considerably more problems with my tennis game than my backhand ever did. Over the years, I spent so much time worrying about what was wrong with my backhand technique that I ultimately developed a phobia about it. I have since learned that I should have focused on what I needed to do and what was good about my backhand. Expending greater mental energy attending to what is good about what we do accelerates growth more than focusing on our weaknesses. This is not to say that we don't learn and grow from our mistakes—absolutely we do—but it has been my experience that learning from what we do well contributes to greater improvement over significantly shorter periods of time.

This is a very powerful tool. Learning to celebrate what is right about ourselves, and the world we live in, is one of the most important mental skills I have learned. It was my father-in-law, Dr. Scott Baird, who really taught me how to apply this principle in achievement. I have seen it reprogram people's lives from the deepest of depression to highest levels of performance. It has immeasurably enhanced my personal life.

Notes

1. www.all-famous-quotes.com/henry_ford_quotes.html
2. Michael J. Gelb, *How to Think Like Leonardo da Vinci: Seven Steps to Genius Every Day* (New York: Dell, 1998), 110.

High Anxiety in Our Society

"Folks are usually about as happy as they make up their minds to be."

—Author unknown

ON A LESS FORTUNATE NOTE, HIGH anxiety is a huge problem in our society. Many adults, and an increasing number of young teenagers, struggle with high anxiety on a daily basis. Drug use, suicide rates, divorce, violent crimes, and bullying behavior are everywhere we turn and are all related in some way to high anxiety. The problem arises from fear—fear of the future in particular. So many of us have set the wrong objectives and expectations, setting ourselves up for high anxiety. Whenever we set outcome objectives, anxiety is heightened, because outcome objectives exist in the future, and no one has direct control over the future.

We all struggle to let go of our worries about what may or may not happen down the road. We worry about financial concerns; we worry about how our children are growing up—whether they will be well liked at school, whether they will grow out of that rebellious stage. We worry about our health, our declining looks as we age, the weight that seems to stick to parts of our body where we don't want it. The list of worries that live in the future is endless, yet this future is imaginary. When we attend to what we have control over, namely the present, anxiety is drastically reduced. Paulo Coelho once wrote in *The Alchemist*, "If you pay attention to the present, you can improve upon it. And, if you improve on the present, what comes later will also be better."[1]

Simply put, think more about what is happening in the present—worry less about the could'ves and should'ves.

Note
1. Paulo Coelho, *The Alchemist* (New York: HarperCollins, 1998), 103.

Attending to Our Side

"I've concluded that some men succeed because they cheerfully pay the price of success. Others, though they may claim ambition and desire, are unwilling to pay that price."

-Wayne Bennett[1]

MANY PEOPLE ARE INSECURE AND UNSURE of themselves. To compensate for these feelings of inadequacy, some people choose to control variables around them in an attempt to feel more safe and secure. These variables are usually other people. However, this behavior only creates a false sense of security. Needless to say, these individuals tend to be less than high performing.

When we delve into other people's business excessively, we open the door to irrelevant stimuli that only serve to lower our ability to function in productive, efficient ways. This energy would be far better channeled into what we can do to improve our performance. I'm not saying that we are not our brother's keeper, but we can only be responsible for what we have control over.

If our brother gets addicted to drugs, it is our responsibility to do everything we can to help, but the choice to take drugs is still our brother's responsibility. We cannot make him do anything he doesn't choose to do. Even in very unpleasant circumstances like this, knowing our parameters, our responsibility, helps us alleviate our anxiety, providing more mental capacity to function and possibly be of greater assistance to our brother.

Here is another tennis analogy that illustrates my point. Tennis can be a very complicated sport when we are always worrying about what our opponent is doing down at the other end of the court. It is draining and not helpful since we don't have direct control over what he or she does. Instead, we need to channel our energy into mastering those variables that lie on our side of the net—those variables that are within our direct control; hence, we should hold ourselves accountable for them.

Moving our feet, hitting with good spin, getting the ball to the right spots, watching the ball, and so forth are a few of the actions we can take to improve our performances. The problem is that many people overlook what can be done because their attention is directed to their opponent's half of the court, and they worry about variables that are outside their control, including things like how their opponent is behaving, the weather, fans, officials, or other irrelevant details.

In game four of the 2007 NBA Western Conference Finals (Utah Jazz vs. San Antonio Spurs), the Jazz self-destructed under pressure and completely lost their composure, meaning their performance dropped off considerably under the pressure that the San Antonio Spurs put on them. Had they been able to stay focused on what they were doing (on their own side of the net) and not let the Spurs impose their will on them (easier said than done, but still it is the only way to perform), they may not have won, but the score would have been a lot closer. Instead, as Deron Williams commented after the series, "Some of the guys were making summer plans. They packed it in." The greatest performers are the ones who perform well over the long run, consistently focusing on their own performances.

At Wimbledon in 2006, after Roger Federer had just beaten Mario Ančić in the quarterfinals, it appeared that no true grass-court players were left in the draw and that Roger would coast to another title. Journeyman Jonas Björkman was Federer's next opponent in the semifinals. At the time, Björkman was thirty-three years old and not the biggest grass-court threat. On the other side of the draw, two baseliners were matching up in the semis—one of them was Rafael Nadal. At the time, Nadal had not proven himself the capable grass-court player he is today. One reporter, like most reporters, was looking for some juicy comments. The reporter seemed to be baiting Federer, making suggestions that he had this tournament in the bag.

However, Federer resisted the reporter's temptations, saying, "I am hitting my forehand very well. I am serving well; if I continue to play like this, things look good for me."[2] Translation: I am very confident in my skills, in particular my forehand and serve (two key components to playing well on grass). If I keep playing like this (acknowledging that he could possibly wake up with a stiff neck or some other bodily dysfunction), things look good for me (again expressing his confidence in the future without allowing his mind to worry about it—at the same time as he isn't putting anyone else down, he is focusing on what he is doing).

We get a glimpse into the fearless mind of a champion by listening carefully to what Federer says. Federer is a disciplined, task-oriented individual, so his anxiety is extremely low, enabling him to focus for long periods on those aspects of performance that he has learned are critical to his performance.

Notes

1. Wayne Bennett, *Don't Die with the Music in You* (Sydney: ABC Books, 2002), 61.
2. CBS news coverage, 2006.

Coaching

I am holding my clients accountable and learning skills to do this even more. I have almost a good handle on my schedule and am working to get everything put into my calendar in a timely fashion. When I continue to coach at this level it is normal to be given additional opportunities and the future looks good for me.

Control What We Can Control

"Our greatest glory consists not in never falling,
but in rising every time we fall."
—Nelson Mandela[1]

I HAVE CONCLUDED, AFTER ANALYZING EVERY aspect of human behavior through the years, that high performers from all walks of life have similar patterns of behavior; or at least they have very similar attitudinal approaches to what they attempt to master. They all seem to deeply understand what they can control and what they can't control.

They work extremely hard to perfect the variables they perceive having control of. They don't waste time and energy directing their attention to the variables they have no control of. I have heard this quote about Michael Jordan several times: "You never beat MJ; sometimes he just runs out of time." MJ never stops trying to figure out the challenge placed before him. He never lets a challenge get him down and he always pushes forward, figuring out what needs to be done.

The biggest objective is to get better. Winning is great—we all want to win—but winning takes care of itself if we keep improving. Many people spend their lives worrying about aspects of their lives or others' lives that they have no control over, creating high levels of anxiety. How fair is it to hold someone accountable for something they couldn't do anything about? Why do we do that to ourselves? We need to learn to evaluate ourselves on those things over which we have control and responsibility. I don't mean the sugar-and-spice do-our-best approach, but the soul-searching am-I-pushing-myself-to-the-limit approach. If we are giving it our absolute best, then we need to relax; that's all we can expect of ourselves.

Becoming Fearless—When using the Mental Skills Journal, simply setting a clear objective and having a plan contributes to feelings of control and lowers anxiety. The journal further directs attention to the positive aspects of our performances, which also lowers anxiety. There is a section in the journal that asks for an evaluation of the day's anxiety level, which encourages greater self-awareness.

Note

1. Quoted in Oliver Goldsmith, *The Works of Oliver Goldsmith*, vol. 4, *The Citizen of the World*, ed. Peter Cunningham (New York: G. P. Putnam's Sons, 1908), 41.

Step 3

CONCENTRATION

International Goals
What can I control
- Taking an action towards it weekly.
- Letting it be known, I want / desire this.
  D.R., Ron + Kate, Bill Sotagy.
- Learn about Switzerland R.E., Check out the
  companies in Lugano & Locarno.
- Finish NLP Training. Get Master Practitioner

Attention Control

"Do not let what you cannot do interfere with what you can do."
　—John Wooden[1]

IN PSYCHOLOGY LITERATURE, CONCENTRATION IS MORE precisely referred to as attentional control, which is defined as being able to attend to relevant stimuli in the environment while not attending to irrelevant stimuli.[2] Relevant or irrelevant stimuli can be either internal or external. Understanding what is relevant and what is irrelevant is critical to high performance.

Theorists have suggested that attention has a significant impact on an athlete's performance. An athlete's ability to attend to appropriate stimuli (relevant cues) during competition has been shown to greatly enhance athletic performance. Achievement goal theorists have suggested that appropriate stimuli (relevant cues) should be task oriented.[3]

Attending to relevant cues allows an athlete to be efficient with mental and physical energy, simplifying the game so that maximum energy can be channeled to those aspects of performance that require high levels of attention. At the same time, the static that surrounds the performance is tuned out or at least turned down, avoiding energy-sapping attention directed to unwanted environmental stimuli.

Attending to irrelevant cues bogs an athlete down with unnecessary information, consuming energy that slows down and complicates the decision making process, making it difficult to make efficient decisions. This is not only energy sapping, it takes the fun out of the game and often results in burnout.

Our control over emotional, mental, and physical energy is paramount to achieve and maintain high performance. A casual observation of human behavior reveals large amounts of wasted mental energy expended on irrelevant cues like worrying about the future, the past, or issues that are not our responsibility (sticking our noses in other people's business or judging others).

These behavior patterns are usually the result of a lack of control over one's emotions. Redirecting our energy to more productive endeavors is not that complicated. Restructuring our objectives and expectations isn't that tricky but involves continuous development of good mental habits. Like losing weight or accomplishing New Year's resolutions, it requires a change in patterns indefinitely and not just for a couple of weeks.

What I mean is that many people fail at weight loss because they go on a diet or exercise for a couple of weeks, months, or even years, lose weight, and then go back to their old habits. Losing weight and keeping it off requires a change of lifestyle—which first requires a change of thought patterns. When we learn to restructure our minds, losing weight or keeping New Year's resolutions becomes nothing more than another achievement objective.

Setting controllable, obtainable objectives and providing feedback each day enables individuals to stay focused daily on the tasks that will help them achieve their objectives. So many people swim around in circles of mediocrity because they don't have a clear purpose in what they are working toward. This is why so many diets and so many New Year's resolutions don't get past the first week. Waking up every morning and writing down our objective for the day, even if it is the same one we have written down for the last six months, helps us refocus and reminds us of what we are working toward. In addition, when we write it down, we feel a greater commitment toward what we want.

The objective is critical; it determines whether we get out of bed in the morning motivated to make a difference in the world, or whether we wake up in the morning and don't want to get out of bed because we have nothing to work toward. Once we set relevant objectives, and we stay focused on them, our energy is directed toward those performance cues that we deem important, thereby allowing us to take control of our lives and our destinies.

The next step, once we have a clear, controllable objective, is to choose two to three specific skill sets to which we can direct our attention. A plan of action for the day enables us to further channel our energy in productive ways to bring our attention to what we can do. It also provides a framework for greater attention to the details of performance. As has been stated, achieving high performance in any area of life requires attention and mastery of the fine details. The minute details are often overlooked by those who struggle with mediocrity.

Setting no more than three action cues a day also provides a framework for the prevention of overanalysis, which can lead to worrying, a major factor in poor attentional control. The most important part of this approach is the consistent use of a daily objective and plan of action. This can be achieved by daily journal writing. Writing in a journal creates greater feelings of commitment and a more objective, honest evaluation of our performance. It is harder to fool ourselves when we write it down.

Anthony Robbins, author and motivational speaker, once said, "One reason so few of us achieve what we truly want is that we never direct our focus; we never concentrate our power. Most people dabble their way through life, never deciding to master anything in particular. In fact, I believe most people fail in life simply because they major in minor things."[4]

Mr. Robbins is saying that we have to commit our focus—our attention—to high performance. We have to make it happen, and that requires honest hard work. Controlling our attention enables us to channel purposeful energy. Mike Brescia, a self-help technology pioneer, said, "Your moods are primarily the result of what you focus on."[5]

John Foster, an English essayist, once said, "He who would do some great thing in this short life must apply himself to the work with such a concentration of his forces, as, to idle spectators, who live only to amuse themselves, looks like insanity."[6]

Further, what most people don't realize is that growth accelerates at a greater rate when we attend to the things we do well. By attending to our previous performance accomplishments, we reinforce skill sets, further ingraining them into our composition while simultaneously increasing our confidence and enhancing our performance. We need to learn from our mistakes, but growth is always more rapid when we train our minds to learn from our strengths first and then our weaknesses. As Brian Tracey has said, "The key to success is to focus our conscious mind on things we desire, not things we fear."[7]

Notes

1.   John R. Wooden, *They Call Me Coach* (Waco, TX: Word Books, 1985), 56.
2.   Craig Manning, "Attentional Control across Performance Levels in Tennis Players" (PhD dissertation, University of Utah, 2007), 1–2; 16.
3.   Ibid., 48.
4.   Anthony Robbins, *Awaken the Giant Within: How to Take Immediate Control of Your Mental, Emotional, Physical and Financial Destiny* (New York: Free Press, 1991), 21.
5.   Mike Brescia, "Hocus Pocus . . . It's All in Your Focus," success-methods.org, 2006 (accessed October 13, 2009).
6.   John Foster, "On Decision of Character," in *The English Essayists: A Comprehensive Selection from the Works of the Great Essayists, from Lord Bacon to John Ruskin*, compiled by Robert Cochrane (Edinburgh: W. P. Nimmo, Hay, & Mitchell, 1887), 335.
7.   briantraceyquotes.wordpress.com.

Attention Control under Pressure

"Tis better to be silent and be thought a fool,
than to speak and remove all doubt."

—**Author unknown**

THEORISTS PROPOSE THAT PRESSURE CAUSES PEOPLE to shift their focus to irrelevant cues. At the highest level of human performance, attention is almost always on what needs to be done, on what is relevant. The highest paid professional baseball player is Alex Rodriguez, who plays for the New York Yankees. He said, "Losers spend all their time worrying about what could happen or what might happen whereas winners focus on what they can do."

Alex Rodriguez had his struggles in 2006 when *Sports Illustrated* writer Tom Verducci wrote an article on baseball's highest paid player and said Rodriguez "could not hit an average fastball, could not swat home runs in batting practice with any regularity, could not field a ground ball or throw from third base with an uncluttered mind and cooperative feet, could not step to the plate at Yankee Stadium without being booed and could not—though he seemed unaware of this—find support in his own clubhouse."[1]

New York is one of the toughest places to perform. The media attention, fan expectations, and owner expectations and involvement—in addition to the large sums that athletes are paid—make New York City a place for only the mentally tough. When Alex was hounded and his abilities were questioned at every turn, his confidence took hit after hit until his production dropped off from its usual high level, resulting in the *Sports Illustrated* article.

The lead-in comments to the article were, "His successes are often overshadowed by his failures. Despite his extraordinary accumulated numbers, New York fans are quick to discount his contributions. And when things go wrong for Alex Rodriguez, even his fellow Yankees find him hard to motivate and harder to understand."[2]

The article goes into detail about how the New York media had been ruthless in evaluating Alex's performances. Even members of his team had been critical. There was talk of him being traded. However, the points from the article that jumped out at me were that no matter how much criticism was directed toward him, Alex consistently channeled his attention to those aspects of his baseball performance that were going well.[3]

At one point during the season, Alex had undergone an alarming amount of criticism that appeared to be taking its toll. Despite this, he still tried to direct his attention toward the positives. As the season moved into the second half, Alex eventually broke out of what the media had labeled a slump and finished the season on a high note, until the playoffs arrived and he again struggled. The following year he came back stronger than ever, performing consistently well throughout the year. I thought this article added further support to what most high-performing athletes do: they consistently focus their mental energy on what is good, on what needs to be done. A fearless mind listens to criticism and then directs attention to what can be done or what needs to be done and does not open the door to self-doubt.

Barry Bonds holds the single-season home run record (2004). Never have teams so avoided one player. Everyone was walking him; opposing managers felt like they had no other choice. Of the 444 pitches thrown at him in one season, "he deemed only 107 good enough to swing at." Of the 107 times he swung the bat, he put 59 balls into play, including 10 home runs. When he was pitched to in the seventh inning in close games, he hit .500 and walked 15 out of 25 times.[4]

Barry Bonds obviously makes good decisions when in the batter's box. He only swings at pitches he knows he can hit. Achieving such high levels of decision making requires incredible attentional control. Further, because teams hardly ever pitch to him, in order to maintain the level of attentional control that is required to perform so highly, during home games Barry goes into the dugout and gets some practice swings to stay alert.

We have all heard about Barry's physical skills, but it is his mental skills that have impressed me. I believe his amazing mental discipline was the leading factor in his astounding performance during 2004. He had people talking about whether it was possible for him to hit .400—the first person to do so since Ted Williams did it in 1941. When asked if he could break the record, he said, "No. Too many pitching changes. . . . I'm not trying to hit .400. I'm just trying to hit."[5] What does this tell us about Barry Bonds's mindset during this period of high performance? He was completely focused on the task at hand.

Notes

1. Tom Verducci, "A-Rod Agonistes," *Sports Illustrated* (September 25, 2006), 37–38.
2. Ibid., 37.
3. Ibid., 37–44.
4. Tom Verducci, "A Season Like No Other," *Sports Illustrated* (May 11, 2004), 54–56.
5. Ibid., 54.

High Performing Athletes

*"Some men are born great, some achieve greatness,
and some have greatness thrust upon them."*
—**William Shakespeare,** *Twelfth Night*[1]

THROUGHOUT MY EXPERIENCES AS AN ATHLETE, coach, and sports psychology consultant, I have come to the conclusion that high-performing athletes don't necessarily do anything special—meaning they do not defy the laws of nature, although it may seem that way at times. When we look closely, the best athletes simply execute the percentages better than most. So in reality, they actually do less.

High-performing athletes are very disciplined at directing their attention to the task at hand and not feeding their own egos. This attention to the details allows them to consistently perform at or near their best while under intense pressure. This is abnormal because the majority of athletes lose their focus under pressure and inadvertently direct their attention to irrelevant cues, resulting in lower levels of performance. The next time you see an outstanding performance in a high-pressure situation like the playoffs, take a close look to see if it is really something out of the ordinary. My bet is that it is the same level of performance achieved in a less pressure-filled situation, like the regular season. It just appears out of the ordinary because everyone else's performance has dropped off under the pressure.

Tom Brady's MVP performances in Super Bowls XXXVI and XXXVIII were amazing. He stayed highly attentive to the task at hand under extreme pressure and executed his play sets with precision. But ask Patriots coach Bill Belichick, and I am sure he will tell us that

Brady just did what he had been doing all season long. The interesting thing is, in both of these games Tom drove the team down the field in the waning moments—not with any gravity-defying moves or superhuman strength, but with poise and tremendous attention to the task at hand.

In both games, it was the kicker, Adam Vinatieri, who kicked the winning field goals. Even Vinatieri's performance was nothing special; he had kicked numerous field goals from that range all year long. But execute a simple task under pressure, and people will be talking about the performance for a while—but remember, we are only as good as our last performance.

Take a look at the averages of professional athletes in any sport. It is rare to find an athlete that has higher averages in the playoffs than in the regular season. And for the few that do have higher averages, it is usually only a slight increase. The statistics show that if we give people enough rope, they will usually hang themselves. I wish this were not the case, but I have seen it happen over and over again. I have experienced this myself on numerous occasions. The ability to maintain high levels of performance for long periods of time is one of man's greatest challenges.

But, if we direct our spiritual, emotional, mental, and physical energy in such a way that brings harmony and balance within ourselves, there is nothing we cannot do. It can be done, it has been done before, and it will be done again. Why not do it now? How we choose to direct our attention is a big component in finding and maintaining a fearless mind.

Note
1. Elizabeth Knowles, ed., *Oxford Dictionary of Quotations* (New York: Oxford, 2004), s.v. William Shakespeare.

Example from *Star Wars*

"Courage is fear holding on a minute longer."
—George S. Patton[1]

I LOVE THE *STAR WARS* MOVIES, although I haven't watched them in years. It was the Jedi knight persona that always drew my attention to the George Lucas films. The Jedi knight epitomizes high-level performance and, specifically, amazing attentional discipline. The Jedi's character is built on his ability to rid himself of the cares of the world to stay attuned to the living Force and thereby react to the surrounding environment with apparent superhuman speed. The Jedi's powers of attentional control are the core of his unique abilities.

It is interesting to me that when Hollywood creates fictional heroes, the central characteristic is often humility. Yet humility is not a characteristic that we commonly strive for in our daily lives. Everywhere I turn, I see males puffing themselves up with false confidence, walking around like they are "all that." I see females walking around with their noses up in the air, pretending that they are somehow superior to others.

I apologize for the negativity, but it concerns me to see people act like they are better than others. Do we need to puff ourselves up with pride to make ourselves feel better? We are all born equals; the worth of everyone's soul is equal. However, what we do at an individual level of performance is not equal. This does not warrant feelings of superiority; it does, however, warrant feelings of confidence and enjoyment—confidence from performing skill sets proficiently, enjoyment at achieving a desired objective. It is not about being better than others. It is about being the best we can be as individuals.

The Jedi is incredibly task-oriented in nature. The Jedi's composure is one of complete calm—except for Anakin Skywalker, who battles with his ego, causing him to struggle with the expectations of the Jedi order. The character trait of a very relaxed, fearless mind enables the Jedi to direct attention to relevant cues in the environment, namely the Force, to be prepared for challenges that may lie ahead.

Becoming Fearless—The use of the Mental Skills Journal directs attention to appropriate stimuli, channeling your energy in an organized, concise way. Set the daily objective and plan of action, evaluate your daily performance by first drawing attention to the positives, and grade your overall attentional focus for the day. It is an incredibly powerful way to channel your energy.

Note

1. Peter G. Tsouras, ed., *The Book of Military Quotations* (St. Paul, MN: Zenith Press, 2005), 102.

Step 4

CONFIDENCE

It's All about Confidence

*"Courage consists, not in blindly overlooking danger,
but in seeing and conquering it."*

—Jean Paul Richter[1]

A FEW YEARS AGO, OUR TENNIS team jumped in the national rankings some twenty-eight places. We started the year ranked forty-nine in the country and finished twenty-one, with a high of fourteen. At the end of that season, we lost our lone senior who had been our number-one player in both singles and doubles. In addition to her leadership on the court, she was our undisputed leader off the court as well. It was a significant loss.

The following year we had an influx of very talented freshmen. One of our players had been ranked as high as 40 in the world and another as high as 55 in juniors, but they weren't even playing one or two. We had a talented sophomore who was our number-one player, so we were young and raw but very talented. Going into the season, I was concerned about who was going to lead the team.

We started off the season on the road in Kansas. Our first match was against Kansas State, a tough opponent on their unique rubber indoor courts in their old field house. Our team struggled through the match, playing the inconsistent, error-filled tennis typical of a young, undisciplined team. One minute they looked brilliant; the next they were shooting themselves in the feet, making mistakes in all kinds of situations.

As the match progressed, I become increasingly annoyed at our self-destructive behavior. With the match tied at 3–all, it came down to one of our players (I will call her Julie) who had been out the entire fall semester with a back and knee injury and was playing her first match back; conditioning was not good.

Julie was very talented, and despite being out for a significant amount of time, she won the first set easily but ran out of steam halfway through the second. Down 4–3 in the third and final set, she was laboring badly. I don't know how she won those three games, other than she was desperately attempting to hang in for the team, hoping to maybe get a third or fourth wind. She had used up her second wind about an hour earlier. I usually didn't give up partway through a match, but in this situation, with our player's health issues, I thought it was all over.

Then something happened that has never happened in all my years of coaching and playing. The player on the opposing team fell while running for a short ball. The moment she went down, I knew it was bad. I got a sick feeling in my stomach. The player had to default. I felt terrible for the young woman, the opposing coach, and the team. They had outperformed us and deserved the victory, but it wasn't as if we could give it to them.

We retreated to a quiet part of the facility, and I let the team have it. I don't do this very often, but I cannot reinforce self-defeating behavior. I don't mind losing, but I cannot tolerate beating ourselves. We left the campus in subdued frames of mind. It was a miserable way to win a match. It is never fun to get ripped on by a coach, and it isn't easy doing the ripping. After regrouping later that night and refocusing our players' minds for the next day's matches, we headed for Lawrence to play the University of Kansas.

The following day we again found ourselves playing tentative tennis. The courts were situated in two rows of four. The top four matches were in a row, and the other two (in collegiate tennis there are six singles matches on at one time) were on the back row of courts. I assigned myself to the front four courts and had my assistant on the back two. We won the doubles point convincingly, which wasn't too much of a surprise with the tremendous doubles talent we had on that team.

As the singles matches got underway, it was apparent that our players were doing their best to execute what we had talked about the previous night. This was a great group of young women, eager to learn. As I was looking down on the top four courts, they were all struggling mightily to find any confidence. We just needed someone to step up and show some assertiveness, to send a message to everyone that we could do this.

These struggles were magnified on court one with our young sophomore (I will call her Leslie). Leslie played as hard as she could, executing our game plan. The points were long, going back and forth until more times than not, Leslie would finally work a short ball. She would step up and miss it, time after time. For those who don't understand, a short ball is what we work for. Missing a short ball is like missing a dunk in basketball, or missing a wide-open goal in soccer. Point after point she would execute her plays, working extremely hard to play the game the right way, and time and time again she would open up the court only to dump the most routine of shots into the net or wide.

I sat by the court dumbfounded. I remember thinking, "Here is a good kid doing everything I asked of her to the best of her ability with all sincerity of heart, only to falter at the last moment." On the changeover I wasn't sure what to say. She was doing everything I had asked of her. She was visibly shaking. We have a word for this phenomenon in athletics. It is called "choking." I was sitting there watching this poor young woman do everything she could to please her demanding coach.

Our player went down 0–5 in a relatively short period of time. To watch the match you would have thought it was much closer or even that Leslie was up, because she was clearly dominating the points; she just couldn't hit a ball in the court to close out the point, no matter how easy the shot was.

Nothing was going well on the other courts either, but they were at least hanging in their sets. The best situation was on court three, where it was 3–2. Our number-one player finally won a game toward the end of the set but turned around the very next game and lost the set very quickly 6–1 (in about twenty minutes). I vividly remember walking off the court after the set to get water from the jug at the back of the court. I leaned against the water jug and thought, "What am I missing? What more is there? She is doing everything I could ask of her; what else is there?"

And then a small voice seemed to whisper to me, "She just needs to believe." I remembered a story about how Steffi Graf, one of the best female tennis players of all time, would tell herself before every break point, "I can do this," over and over again, flooding her mind with positive thoughts so that no negative thoughts could enter her mind. I went back out onto the court. The changeover finished. Leslie was already heading back onto the court to start the second set, and I still hadn't gotten her any water.

I ran up to her and gave her the water and said, "Don't talk, just listen." I told her she was doing everything perfect. I said, "Keep doing exactly what you are doing." She looked at me like I was crazy. She had just lost the set 6–1 in record time. I told her, "All you need to do is to believe in yourself." I told her I wanted her to tell herself after every point, "I can do this, I can do this." I went back to my spot on the bench and watched as Leslie played a great point just like she had been: stepping in, hitting strong balls to the corners until she got the short ball. As she stepped up, I think I held my breath, but this time she made the short ball, and instead of hitting an approach shot off of it, she hit it cleanly enough for it to be a winner.

Leslie continued to make her shots and ended up winning the first game easily. On the first changeover up 1–0, I quickly told her Steffi Graf's story as briefly as I could while she walked from one side of the court to the other. Strangely, she didn't act like I was crazy, but to this day I still think I must have looked like an idiot running around the court like crazy. The following two games were comprised of long points, with both players hitting and moving very well. Leslie continued to make her shots, even the short balls that had previously eluded her.

I was honestly surprised with the amazing turnaround. I tried to act like I knew what I was doing, but this was all a learning experience for me. After winning the third game in a row, she came and sat down on the changeover. I asked her, "So are you telling yourself you can do it after each point?" She responded with an assertive, "No." I was initially annoyed. I thought I had actually learned an important lesson about confidence. Then she followed up with, "I am not saying it after every point; I am saying it after every shot." I was surprised. I didn't know how she could hit and move while talking to herself, but who was I to argue? She was playing great.

It was as if the simple phrase "I can do it" being repeated over and over again was a shot of confidence straight to the bloodstream. If we could package this phenomenon, it would be more valuable than steroids. By repeating the phrase over and over, Leslie didn't allow any self-doubt or hesitation into her thought patterns, and it resulted in a calm, smooth, assertive athlete. The transformation was awesome. I had never witnessed the amazing effect confidence could have on someone.

By the fourth game, Leslie was really starting to heat up. She won the next game at love (meaning without losing a point). I got a little excited; okay, I got very excited. I jumped up and ran to all three of the other courts under my responsibility. We still were not ahead on any of these courts, but we weren't out of any of them either. Nobody was playing great, and all three of the players seemed to be struggling with tentativeness as well. I told each of them the same story about Steffi Graf.

I had to wait for the changeover to talk to our players, so by the time I got to all three and back to Leslie, it must have taken about fifteen to twenty minutes. As I got back to court one to check on her progress, Leslie was sitting down on another changeover. I went up to her and asked, "How is it going?" She said, "Good." I asked what the score was, and she responded with 6–1. I told her to keep it up, and I left to go back to the other players. On two of the three other courts, we were able to pull out convincing wins after the slow start in the first set. Our player on court four lost her first set but seemed to be getting stronger.

After spending a little more time with our number-four player to help her get off to a better start in the second set, I went back to our number-one girl. When I got back to her court, I watched her play a point that she ended up losing. She then hit the balls down to the other end of the court, meaning she just lost that game. She seemed relaxed, so I was confident that things were still going well despite the loss of the game.

I stayed where I was, watching her play great tennis and win the next game. I moved out onto the court to meet her for the changeover and was surprised to see her walk straight to the net and shake hands with her opponent. The match was over. Upon getting post-match feedback, I learned that the one game I had seen her lose was the only game she lost in that third set. So she had lost the first set 1–6, then won the next two sets 6–0, 6–1. I have never forgotten this match and have used it many times as an example of the power of believing.

Further, it never appeared to me that her opponent ever let up. She appeared to play long, strong points throughout the entire match. As a point of interest, we won easily on two of the other three courts, hardly dropping a game after believing more in ourselves. We won the match on court four, but in three sets. That player was always a little stubborn.

This match was a turning point in our season. From that point on, we exhibited significantly more confidence in ourselves, pulling out wins in several close 4–3 matches and finishing with another conference tournament title and an NCAA berth. All we had needed was that belief in ourselves and in what we were doing.

I have since learned that we cannot have too much confidence. In fact, I feel we all need to store as much confidence as possible for those tough moments that we all encounter. That being said, every time an opportunity arises that we can build more confidence, we need to take advantage of it. After all, no one can give us confidence; we have to find it ourselves.

Notes

1. John P. Bradley, Leo F. Daniels, and Thomas C. Jones, comps., *The International Dictionary of Thoughts: An Encyclopedia of Quotations from Every Age for Every Occasion* (Chicago: J. G. Ferguson, 1969), s.v. "Courage."

Importance of Confidence

"Whatever the mind of man can conceive and believe, it can achieve."
—Napoleon Hill[1]

CONFIDENCE IS ACCLAIMED AS THE MOST critical psychological characteristic influencing sports performance.[2] In addition, it is reported to be the most consistent factor distinguishing highly successful from less successful athletes.[3] Confidence is defined as "a feeling or belief that one can rely on someone or something."[4]

Self-confidence is defined as "a feeling of trust in one's abilities, qualities, and judgment."[5] Belief is defined as "an acceptance that a statement is true or that something exists."[6] To me, general confidence is of greater significance because so much of what we do in life is not so much about ourselves as it is about trusting in the laws of nature, the law of averages. Therefore, evaluating one's overall confidence is of greater value than evaluating self-confidence.

Confidence is saying, "If I hit the ball with this much spin, gravity will bring it down." It doesn't matter how fast, or how intelligent, or how talented we are. If we don't have any confidence, the rest doesn't matter.

Notes
1.   Napoleon Hill, "Napoleon Hill—What the Mind Can Conceive, Believe, and Achieve," video recording, www.scholarspot.com.
2.   Robin S. Vealey et al., "Sources of Sport-Confidence: Conceptualization and Instrument Development," *Journal of Sport and Exercise Psychology* 20, no. 1 (1998), 54–80.
3.   J. Graham Jones, *Stress and Performance in Sport*, edited by Lew Hardy (New York: J. Wiley, 1990).

4.   *The New Oxford American Dictionary,* s.v. "Confidence."
5.   Ibid., s.v. "Self-confidence."
6.   Ibid., s.v. "Belief."

Confidence and Arrogance

"Obstacles don't have to stop you. If you run into a wall, don't turn around and give up. Figure out how to climb it, go through it, or work around it."

—Michael Jordan[1]

I ONCE HAD AN ATHLETE (I will call her Anna) who was immensely talented but at the strangest of times would engage in self-destructive behavior. At least I thought it was at the strangest of times. It has been my observation that most of us engage in self-destructive behavior when things are not going well. We have a tendency as humans to make things a lot worse than they need to be. Anna was self-destructive when everything appeared to be going great. She would get on these rolls where she would play disciplined, smart tennis and win eight to ten matches in a row. Then she would play a match where she would completely implode.

After tracking this pattern in her performance for a while, I brought this to her attention, and we discussed what was going on in her head. My mentor once said we have got to get to the issues beneath the issues. I have found this advice to be incredibly accurate. Many times the individuals themselves do not know what is holding them back, and their troublesome behavior is usually just the symptom and not the root of the problem. Anna was no different. She didn't know why she would do this, but she did know something wasn't quite right.

Upon probing this particular athlete in an attempt to get to the issues beneath the issues, it became clear what her problem was. It is amazing how one inappropriate thought can cause such destructive behavior. Anna made the comment that she was afraid of becoming overly confident and thus becoming arrogant. I remember her comment so clearly because it caught me by surprise. I was so impressed with the quality of her character.

I told her I wanted to think about what she had said overnight. I was pretty sure I knew what needed to be done, but I thought her sincere concern for not wanting to be a jerk and treat people inappropriately deserved careful consideration. I went home and did some research while pondering over her mental state. The answer did not change, but the difference between confidence and arrogance did have more meaning to me than it had previously.

This is my interpretation of confidence and arrogance. Confidence (assertiveness) and arrogance (aggressiveness) are two completely separate entities, mutually exclusive. However, many people jump back and forth from confident thinking to arrogant thinking. As mentioned in the motivation chapter, confidence is an "I am good" approach without any comparison to others, just a belief in oneself. Confidence can stand the test of time because it is not dependent on anyone or anything. Confident people create skills, services, and products.

Arrogance is an "I am good, you stink" approach. Arrogance is dependent upon comparison to another, on being better than others, or putting others down. Arrogant individuals do not spend time developing their skill sets and building their confidence. They don't create; they tear down. The better we all get at ridding ourselves of arrogance, and the more energy we put into performing specified skill sets to help lift up ourselves and others, the better this world will be.

I don't believe that once we reach a certain level of confidence we automatically become arrogant. As long as we think the right way, confidence can be built indefinitely. However, arrogance is something we all need to beware of every day. We may not automatically switch from confidence to arrogance at a certain level, but arrogant thinking can, at any point along the journey of life, become a bad habit. If we are not aware of what we are doing, what we are thinking, and what we are saying, we can all too quickly fall into the pit of arrogant thoughts and, ultimately, the cycle of mediocrity.

The following day I met Anna, and we talked about the difference between confidence and arrogance (and cockiness for that matter). We talked about staying confident by attending to the task at hand, the performance cues that were within her direct control. If she did this, there would be no limit to the confidence she could obtain. Anna went on to develop a high level of confidence. She became quite fearless and had an amazing college career, but more important, she became successful no matter what she did.

Another story to illustrate the significance of arrogance occurred when I was working with a young tennis player a few years ago. He was only fourteen, and we had been working on good decision making for a period of time. I had been preaching to him that he was only as good as the decisions he made, that it was not him that made him special, it was what he did. I was attempting to teach him that high performance requires constant attention.

One summer workout, I got one of the players from the tennis team who was teaching camps to play a set against this young man. The young man started out hot, making great decisions and executing the fundamentals of tennis. His performance level was especially high for someone his age. This resulted in him winning the first three games: up 3–0. After he won the third game, I noticed a distinct change in his body language, in particular his walk. As he walked around the net, his body language reeked of arrogance.

I thought to myself, "Here we go, let's see what happens here." If I were a betting man, I would have put my house on his performance dropping off. The first point in the fourth game, he attempted to smack the ball down the line off the return of the serve for a winner (a very low percentage shot). The ball hit halfway up the net. A bad miss. The body language was predictable. His shoulders slumped a little, basically sending the message, "I thought I was good enough to make that shot."

He walked to the other side for the next point. Bang—another wail down the line. The ball hit a third of the way up the net this time, an even worse miss. His shoulders slumped even further, starting to communicate feelings of self-pity after only two poor decisions (it's very difficult to maintain confidence when making poor decisions). Third point—wham! Another attempted return down the line; this time the ball actually hit the ground before it hit the net. He then proceeded to hit the extra ball in his pocket out of the court and start whining and complaining that he hated this game and didn't want to play anymore.

I started laughing to myself, not at him directly, but at people as a whole. It is amazing how fast we go from confidence to self-pity. He started out focusing on the task at hand (the skills), and he was able to do what he set out to do, building confidence rapidly. Then, after he had won the first three games, his thought processes made the dreaded switch from task orientation to ego orientation. Why do we do this? I believe it goes back to pride.

Benjamin Franklin once said, "There is perhaps no one of our natural passions so hard to subdue as pride. Disguise it, struggle with it, beat it down, stifle it, mortify it as much as one pleases, it is still alive and will every now and then peep out and show itself." Franklin quipped that even if he were to overcome his pride, he would probably be proud of his humility.[2]

It has been my observation that those who have been able to discipline themselves to stay focused on the task (humility) always seem to perform better for longer. After the three games, this young man switched his focus from attending to the task at hand (humility) to thinking he was "the man" (ego/pride/arrogance). His attention was not on the present. Hence, good decision making went out the window, and the poor decisions led to badly executed shots. High performance is all about using the laws of nature to our advantage. It's about putting the percentages in our favor. High performance is not about trying to be a superhero; it's not attempting to defy the laws of nature.

Another lesson to be learned from this young man's arrogant behavior is not so much that he made bad decisions—we all make poor decisions every day—but that we need to have the humility to take responsibility for our decisions. We don't knowingly make risky decisions and then throw a tantrum when the low percentages don't return favorable results. To be high performing, we have to always know what we are doing. We must always have a clear objective; we must always be responsible for our choices.

It is our life, our performance. There is a time and a place to take a risk; life would be boring if we always played it safe, so taking a risk is good from time to time. But accept the consequences of both the positive and negative results. When the consequences are negative, take it like a warrior. Don't complain you didn't know what you were doing. We should always know. Ignorance is no excuse.

The truly confident high-performing athletes are assertive and completely in control of their environments. Self-mastery doesn't have to come at the expense of others, but there is no room for any passive, self-defeating behavior either.

A couple of years ago during practice, we were inside playing points out. I was pushing our players hard to attend to getting better and to the performance cues that would accelerate their development. About halfway through, something amazing happened without any real warning (those who weren't looking for it probably wouldn't have noticed it). For about three rotations (so for about fifteen minutes), the team executed their skill sets almost to perfection. The tennis for this group of individuals was amazing for this brief period of time. Who knows who actually won; it did not matter. It was just practice, but for a moment it was fun to watch human beings performing at an incredibly high level.

I know it's just tennis, but we need to celebrate these moments. Our team was almost perfect. I stopped everybody after a while, knowing that I probably ruined the rhythm, but I wanted to reinforce the moment, to celebrate what was right about what we were doing. I brought everyone to the middle of the building, and I told them that this was why we do all this training, the brutal conditioning, the footwork drills every day, the intense practices, the mental training before we ever hit a ball. This is why we make so many sacrifices. We do it for self-mastery; nothing is more fulfilling and rewarding. I can still feel the chills going down my spine that I felt that day. There was no one else in the building but those on the team. For me it was one of the highlights of the season.

Human mastery—how wonderful it is. It only comes now and then, and its moments can be fleeting, but once we have experienced that feeling of doing something really well, we cannot get enough of it. It is like a drug. We want more of it, and we want it as often as possible. When we get that chill down our spine, we know that something special is happening. These moments are worth everything we can give. And that is what they require—our very best effort for long periods of time.

Notes

1. thinkexist.com.
2. Quoted in Alex Tresniowski, *Tiger Virtues: 18 Proven Principles for Winning at Golf and in Life*, (Philadelphia: Running Press, 2005), 54.

Cockiness and Passiveness

For whosoever exalteth himself shall be abased;
and he that humbleth himself shall be exalted.

—Luke 14:11

AFTER SPENDING SIGNIFICANT TIME PONDERING OVER confident (assertive) versus arrogant (aggressive) behavior, I turned my attention to cockiness. Cockiness to me is belief in oneself and telling everyone about it. I personally have never had a problem with cocky people. In fact, I had some friends growing up who were pretty darn cocky. It has never been my chosen approach to life, but everyone to their own. The reason I don't mind cockiness is there is no comparison with others. Cocky individuals are not trying to put others down as arrogant individuals do; they are simply trying to build themselves up. How could that ever be bad? It might be annoying, but not bad.

The next mental attribute that needs mentioning is passiveness. A passive individual has an "I am not good, you are great" attitude. These individuals put themselves down by thinking others are superior to them in some way. Why do they do this? It seems that for some, life appears to be very difficult. Although it isn't apparent on the surface, passive individuals struggle with outcome thinking. They consistently evaluate themselves on the outcome, setting themselves up for failure. The problem with passive individuals is, when they allow an aggressive individual to take advantage of them, resentment builds under the surface. Everyone has a breaking point, and when pushed far enough, this resentment comes out at some point. Often this buildup of resentment is expressed as some form of self-destructive behavior. Further, passive individuals seldom maintain any sort of mental attention in the present.

Because they think so little of themselves, they always perceive others as better than they are. They consistently dwell on the future and the past. The mind is jumping all over the place, further heightening performance that is less than desirable. Those individuals who feel they do not have control over their lives often find others who share similar feelings. They exemplify the old adage "misery loves company."

For many years I have taught that the only way to help someone engaging in self-defeating behavior is to not sugarcoat things. Honesty is very important. When we sugarcoat others' behavior, we become partially responsible for their behavior since we are reinforcing their self-pity.

The following story illustrates my point. A few years back I coached a player (I will call her Nancy) who allowed her emotions to dictate her attitudes and her behaviors. Twice in the preseason I had addressed Nancy's tendency to feel sorry for herself when things didn't go exactly as she wanted on the tennis court. Nancy got off to a great start during the regular season, winning her first ten matches (five singles and five doubles). Whether on the court or off, she was happy, bubbly, bouncing off the walls. Nancy was playing number five singles for us at the time (six singles players play in collegiate tennis).

Nancy then lost a close match to a strong player from a nationally ranked team. It was high-level tennis. Then she lost a second match to another strong player; again the level of tennis was quite high. Then Nancy lost another, and it was evident that her game had started to drop off with her confidence. She was no longer bouncing off the walls when I passed her in the halls. After her fourth loss in a row, we switched her to sixth in the lineup. The girl who had been playing sixth was now simply playing better than Nancy.

The fifth match we played was with Notre Dame, a traditionally strong women's tennis team. We played them at home and found ourselves down 2–3 when our fifth and sixth singles players started their matches (we have only four indoor courts, and the fifth and sixth matches play when the courts open up, making for climactic endings at times). Our number-five player got started a little sooner than Nancy, playing sixth. Our number-five won her match comfortably, tying the match at 3–3 with everything coming down to Nancy. We ended up losing the match 3–4, which was not as disappointing as how we lost. Nancy lost 6–0, 6–0. Our player tanked the match, meaning she didn't even try.

From a coach's perspective, that is pretty much the greatest mistake a player can make. I didn't say anything after the match. We did a quick evaluation of the match, and I let the team go. I told them I would see them on Tuesday, like we often do at that time of year, and we would evaluate the match in more detail. Tuesday morning I was in my office when Nancy came in. She apologized for her lack of effort. She obviously felt bad.

I felt strongly, though, that if I didn't hold her accountable for her poor effort, she would engage in this self-defeating behavior again. She had been counseled about self-destructive behavior on two prior occasions. What if she engaged in this type of behavior off the tennis court, perhaps in her marriage or her career? Or what if she modeled this behavior to her children, perpetuating behaviors that can prevent us from achieving our objectives and reaching our dreams?

I informed her that she would not be playing for a while. She was shocked because at that point in the season we did not have any other players. We had sustained two season-ending injuries to our best two players and did not have anyone else on our roster. Nancy left my office mad at me, but I thought that was better than her feeling sorry for herself. I then asked a young woman to come and play for us who had worked out on the team in the preseason but had chosen to focus on school because it didn't appear she was going to get much, if any, playing time once the season got into full swing.

Fortunately she accepted, and although she had not played in months, she fought hard. In her first match she lost easily, but it was to a strong player from the University of Tennessee whose team was ranked seven in the country at the time. After the match, Nancy came up to me and said, "Okay, I have learned my lesson. I won't get down on myself again. I want to play." I told her I was glad she had learned her lesson, but I still was not going to play her just yet. Our new player played another six matches for us before straining her knee. She had obviously fallen out of match condition, and the wear and tear from match competition took a toll on her body.

I decided to put Nancy back in the lineup. She played hard throughout the rest of the season, focusing on her performance and not worrying about winning and losing. Nancy kept her head up the whole time whether playing well or having a rough day. She closed out the remainder of the season winning her last five matches. Although this season had a happy ending, the lesson was not ingrained well enough. The following year she continued to struggle with concerns about things outside her direct control and had a major meltdown on a road trip, resulting in her being sent home.

Eventually Nancy decided not to continue her tennis at BYU, mainly, I believe, because she couldn't handle the pressure I put on her to take responsibility for herself and her performance. This experience was a great learning opportunity for me. It helped me to have a clearer understanding of what tough love is all about. Further, we are the only ones who can stop ourselves from achieving our dreams. Self-destructive behavior should not be perpetuated by ourselves or condoned by those responsible for others. The behavior won't change if it keeps getting sugarcoated.

Developing Confidence

"Strength does not come from physical capacity.
It comes from an indomitable will."
   —Mahatma Gandhi[1]

SINCE CONFIDENCE IS ACCLAIMED AS THE most critical psychological characteristic influencing sports performance,[2] it probably would be wise for us to know how to develop confidence. Research has shown there are four primary modes that build confidence: previous performance accomplishments; vicarious experiences; verbal persuasions; and physiological states.[3]

Previous performance accomplishments: Confidence is accumulated when we learn and reinforce what we have done well in the past. Confidence and skill sets can be developed very quickly when we learn from our strengths.

Vicarious experiences: Learning from others is a powerful tool for developing skill sets and confidence. It is assumed that we all have the same nervous system; therefore, if someone else can perform a skill so can we. Modeling the behavior of others is often one of the quickest ways to learn skills.

Verbal persuasion: The brain's neuropathways are programmed by what we communicate to ourselves most often. Repeatedly telling ourselves we can do something is another powerful tool to developing confidence.

Physiological states: Being able to control our bodies so they function as we desire further enhances confidence.[4]

These four components, when utilized consistently, can enhance confidence rapidly. I have seen many athletes improve their confidence in a short period of time when incorporating these principles. The Mental Skills Journal incorporates the first and last two methods for developing confidence. When used correctly, the journal stimulates growth in confidence by reinforcing three things that were performed well that day and choosing one aspect of the day's performance that could be improved (previous performance accomplishments).

The journal simultaneously perpetuates positive self-talk by stimulating positive self-assessment of the daily performance (verbal persuasion). Further, the journal stimulates honest self-assessment of the day's actions (physiological states). The only confidence-building skill not directly addressed in the Mental Skills Journal is learning vicariously, and that is easily overcome by utilizing the daily notes section to write down any skills learned from observing others.

There are multiple benefits to incorporating high levels of confidence. Everything from athletics to parenting to social relations is affected by confidence or a lack of it. Research has shown that confidence does the following:

- Arouses positive emotions
- Facilitates concentration
- Increases effort and persistence
- Affects game strategies
- Influences motivation

Confidence can take an individual with nonexistent skill sets and make them respectable; ordinary skill sets and make them good; and incredible skill sets and make them great.

Notes
1. Mahatma Gandhi, *All Men Are Brothers: Life and Thoughts of Mahatma Gandhi as Told in His Own Words* (New York: Columbia University Press, 1958), 105.
2. Robin S. Vealey et al., "Sources of Sport-Confidence: Conceptualization and Instrument Development," *Journal of Sport and Exercise Psychology* 20, no. 1 (1998), 54–80.
3. Albert Bandura, "Self-efficacy: Toward a Unifying Theory of Behavioral Change," *Psychological Review* 84, no. 2 (1977), 191–215.
4. Ibid.

The Power of
Positive Thinking

"I believe in every shot I hit that I can pull it off. It's just, I guess, my mind-set. I've always believed that."
—Tiger Woods[1]

LARRY IS ONE OF THE MOST amazingly high-performing individuals I have ever met. I love spending time with him because his energy and enthusiasm for life make him so much fun to be around. One night I was setting up chairs with Larry for a church service the following morning. It was late, and we both had wives waiting for us at home. As we were leaving the church building, all I was thinking about was getting home and having hot chocolate (it was wintertime).

As we were getting into our cars, Larry turned to me and said, "We are so blessed. Check out that setting." I looked in the direction he was pointing; the sight was amazing with the lights in the valley below. It looked awesome with the moon over the lake. It was a setting I had seen many times but hadn't really noticed. Larry went on to express how lucky we are to live where we live. I remember getting home and talking to my wife about the beautiful setting that night. It was a simple thing, but it's something Larry always does. He is always high on life, always looking at what's right about the world. But he wasn't always like that.

Growing up, Larry suffered from ADHD. As a child he was put on medication to help control the chemical imbalances. He talks about how his high school days were a blur, how he would basically be in a daze all day and then crash the moment he got home. Then one day at the age of twenty-five, he was working as a bellboy at the local Marriott hotel. A man who couldn't have been much older than Larry, with obvious wealth, was checking out of his room and wanted help with his bags. Larry asked him how he had become so successful. The man did not say much but pulled out a book on positive affirmations and gave it to Larry.

The book talked about how each day we need to spend fifteen minutes programming our minds for success. How powerful it is to visualize success, to create positive thought processes. Larry started each morning while he was shaving telling himself over and over again, "I love my wife, I love my life, I love my job, I love where I live," and so forth. He also would visualize himself driving the car he wanted to own and, more important, what he needed to do in order to own the car of his dreams. A short time later, Larry was off his medication and functioning better than ever. He would still have a day here or there when he would get down, but this was becoming less frequent.

Overcoming the chemical imbalance he was born with through sheer force of will and confidence is an impressive feat. This fruit from developing a fearless mindset resulted in Larry increasing his income from $1,500 a month to over $20,000 a month. He has never earned a degree from a university, but through the power of positive thoughts and actions he has become a shining example of a high-performing individual. Sometimes we spend too much time attempting to figure out how to do something rather than just believing we can do it. I love spending time with Larry; it is uplifting just being in his presence.

Becoming Fearless—The Mental Skills Journal provides the opportunity to build confidence by encouraging the evaluation of previous performance accomplishments each day. When you write down what you did well and what you want to do better, you build your own confidence.

Note

1.   Alex Tresniowski, *Tiger Virtues: 18 Proven Principles for Winning at Golf and in Life*, (Philadelphia: Running Press, 2005), 64.

Step 5

DECISION MAKING

The Answer

"Courage is not the absence of fear, but rather the judgment that something else is more important than fear."
—**Ambrose Redmoon**[1]

WHEN I BECAME THE HEAD WOMEN'S tennis coach at BYU, my philosophy was to help the players on the team however I could. I worked hard at doing this, getting to work early, not taking a lunch break, utilizing every allowable hour (per NCAA rules) to work with the women on the team. We had some immediate success taking the team from not being ranked in the preseason to a high of thirty-two and making it to the conference title match.

The following year we were fortunate enough to win a conference title and continued to climb the national rankings. In my third year we had internal problems and did not have a good, nor enjoyable, year. In my fourth year we lost our top two players to season-ending injuries and illnesses before the season had barely gotten underway. But we still managed to get to the conference finals, pulling out some solid wins to get there. I was happy with what we accomplished, but even with what we had that year, it still felt like we were going around in circles.

I remember at the time going through an in-depth, soul-searching analysis of our actions, plans, and activities. Every aspect of our program was analyzed, breaking it down to its smallest parts. Upon completing the self-evaluation of our program, I found that we were doing everything the top programs were doing from a physical standpoint. We worked on the physical components just as the other top programs did. Although tennis can be extremely annoying at times in our attempts to master the game, it is not rocket science, and any good coach can teach how to hit a ball over the net.

Condition-wise, our players were in good shape, although I did notice some room for improvement in this department. Better conditioning would help, but it didn't feel like that was the key to higher performance. Conditioning is the norm in this day and age—the status quo. Gone are the days when we can outperform opponents simply because we can outlast them. Everybody does yoga, Pilates, footwork drills, weight lifting, and so forth. If we're not doing those things, we're not competing on equal ground.

We also utilized a nutritionist to educate the team on how to eat appropriately; some of our players listened and worked hard to take good care of their bodies, while others didn't do such a good job. A sports psychologist helped us deal with problems as they arose. These problems ranged from eating disorders to homesickness. I felt that all things being equal from a physical standpoint, the mental side was the key to taking our performance to new heights.

I believe in performance enhancement and studied various systematic approaches. I decided to take a more assertive approach to our team's performance from a psychological perspective. Around this time, the professor of one of my sports psychology classes gave a lesson on random versus blocked training. Random training implies practicing like it is a real match, simulating real-match situations. Blocked training is practicing a specific skill in a controlled, almost laboratory setting. An example of blocked training in tennis would be feeding balls from a basket the same way repeatedly. It is good for developing a stroke, but has little real-match value.

Random practice would involve simulating a real point, where the ball almost never comes at us the same way, and point playing is a very good simulation of real-match situations. Research tells us that while blocked practice skill sets are acquired more rapidly, retention is not reliable under pressure as in match situations. In random practice, on the other hand, skill sets are not learned as quickly, but the retention is more reliable under the pressure of match situations.[2] As I reviewed this information, it reminded me about a concern I had had throughout my whole career.

What is the point in training so hard on our strokes, footwork, and conditioning if we can't perform under pressure? Much of our training is a waste of time if we don't have control over our mental processes in pressure situations. I started analyzing everything we did to see if it had real-match benefits. After that fourth year, I changed everything we did to focus on what would help us to perform better in matches. Every drill we did that year had a mental component. In addition, we started doing mental skills training, namely visualization, before every practice.

I would go over what we wanted to work on that day, isolating specific areas; then I would do a visualization session, utilizing imagery to go over, in detail and in real time, those skill sets identified. During these sessions I would direct our players' attention to what they needed to do to perform the skills in a desirable way. A large part of this process was directed toward where to hit the ball rather than always focusing on how to hit the ball.

My theory was that the physical aspects of tennis were important for hitting the ball, but deciding where to hit the ball (decision making) is of greater significance than anything else. My coach on the pro tour always said, "The worst hit shot to the right spot is better than the best hit shot to the wrong place." We worked hard on decision making the whole year. I promised myself that every player I worked with from that point on would know exactly what they were trying to do at all times.

It is tempting to focus on a formula for performance and not worry about reading the surrounding conditions and making appropriate adjustments. I have worked with many tennis players who find a new physical skill that helps them to hit the ball better, like "staying down on their shots."

It is easy to fall into the trap of thinking that staying down will make them great—that staying down will guarantee them success. The truth is, staying down probably helps in hitting the ball better, but without knowing where to hit the ball, staying down will not get us very far. In the end, all the physical skills in the world are useless if we don't know what to do with them. High performance demands our very best mental skills all the time. As soon as we think we have it, we lose it.

After I came to this realization about decision making, every drill was done with a strategic plan in mind. The previous year we had gone

12–11. After making major changes to our training program (with the same schedule as the year before) we went 22–6. The year following that, we went 22–4, and so on. I was stunned with the difference, but every day I saw the advantages to working on decision making. Since then I have continued to teach the athletes I work with that the key to high performance is consistently making good decisions. Several times there have been struggles when I have moved a little too far away from the underlying philosophy of mental skills.

When we are always striving to improve, it is important to remember the foundation on which our system is built. In 2007–08 we had a very interesting season. For a number of years we had approached high performance in basically the same way; each year we had isolated a couple of things we wanted to do better, but the system had remained quite constant, and accordingly the results were favorable. We had won three of the last four conference tournaments (and may have won the other one if we had not been struck with massive injuries at the end of one season).

The 2007-08 season was different from all the other years. As we got our system down and the individuals that played and worked for us built confidence in the system, a lot of our involvement in the training process decreased. The young ones that we brought into our program largely learned from the older ones. In our situation, our junior and senior players modeled the type of behavior expected of our freshmen and sophomores. This year our three seniors were out with injuries during the fall, and we had no juniors on the team, so we really had no one to model the kind of confidence and behavior that breeds high performance.

These new players were trying to live up to the expectations of previous teams without the leadership and example of seasoned veterans. On top of that, the coaching staff wanted to take the program's performance level to new heights and decided to focus on some intricate details of high performance. We pushed these new players hard; the problem was that we were treating them like seasoned veterans, mistakenly assuming that they already had the fundamentals down. This was a great lesson for me. Sometimes we get so busy trying to reach new heights of performance that we forget the fundamentals that make up 80 to 90 percent of what we do.

After a minor analysis of what we were doing, I realized that our practices were focusing on skill sets that made up maybe 10 percent of the game. We assumed these players knew and understood the other 90 percent of fundamentals, or at least they had them down to a degree that they were ready to move on. Sometimes we get so busy trying to develop the skills we don't have that we forget about the skills we do have.

For a while I felt we were going around in circles again. The players on the team were trying their best but were confused and lost, and they didn't feel confident about what they were doing. It is frustrating to lose perspective in what we are trying to accomplish, especially since I am supposed to be an expert in human performance. But if we don't fall off the path of high performance at times, then I don't believe we are pushing ourselves hard enough. Only those willing to take risks learn new skill sets that can be the difference between being really good and being great.

It seems apparent that each time my performance or my team's performance drops off, it is because we have been experimenting with something new. The old adage "one step back to go two steps forward" is very real, although I would say it is one step back to go many steps forward. Not many people have the guts to sacrifice performance in the present for improved performance in the future. Sure, they want to get better, but they are not willing to pay the price. Tiger Woods has rebuilt his swing twice since he has risen to the top of the golfing world. Now that is fearless.

Notes

1. Steve Chandler, *Fearless: Creating the Courage to Change the Things You Can* (Bandon, OR: Robert Reed, 2008), 17.
2. Dr. Barry Schultz, University of Utah, Exercise Science Department, motor learning class, 2005.

Why Is Decision Making So Important?

"Ninety-five percent of performance is physical, five percent is mental. However, the five percent that is mental rules the other ninety-five percent."

—Dr. Keith Henschen[1]

NO INDIVIDUAL IS DESTINED FOR GREATNESS. We achieve high performance only through hard work—and not just any work, but precise work, paying attention to specific details of performance. High performance is achieved only through a fearless mind.

To further support the importance of decision making, we need to take a look at the nature of confidence. Confidence can be very unstable; it cannot be maintained over long periods of time without making good decisions. For example, if a basketball player continually shoots the ball with a defender in his face, he eventually loses confidence over time. The law of averages tells us that a defender in a shooter's face results in a lower shooting percentage than shooting wide open. Hence, confidence is dependent on good decision making.

Good decision making, however, is not dependent on confidence. If we watch athletics closely, we notice that when athletes are confident, they tend to make good decisions. When they are confident, their anxiety is usually lower, resulting in better concentration and better decision making. Also, when anxiety is low, individuals are less likely to panic and rush. However, when athletes are not confident, they often make rash, panicky decisions. I have seen athletes in numerous situations struggling with low confidence either because they have been in a slump or because they are coming back from injury.

It is interesting that individuals who don't beat themselves up tend to regain their confidence more rapidly. When we make good decisions, we make fewer mistakes, and when we make fewer mistakes, we are more likely to perform more assertively—resulting in enhanced performance. When overall performance is enhanced for extended periods of time, the law of averages tells us we will eventually win. The more we win, the greater our confidence and the more likely we will relax and not rush, further enhancing good decision making.

The moment our egos get the better of us is the moment we lose focus on what we are doing. When our attention is motivated by our egos, we lose focus on what needs to be done from one moment to the next, and good decision making goes out the window. A favorite saying of mine is, "We are only as good as the decisions that we make"— meaning that as soon as we stop making decisions based on the reality of the moment, our performance diminishes rapidly. High performance is dependent on making the best decision at the time.

Notes
1. Favorite saying of author's mentor, Dr. Keith Henschen, sports psychology professor, Exercise Science Department, University of Utah.

Decision making Experiences

"The worst hit shot to the right spot is better than the best hit shot to the wrong place."
—Barry Phillips-Moore[1]

I REMEMBER A PARTICULAR TOURNAMENT WHERE I was the number-two seed. When I checked the draw, I recognized the name of the person I would play in the first round as a guy I knew well (he had never been great but had a lot of potential). He used to train in my uncle's squad before moving to a different city. I hadn't seen him for a while, but he always had great strokes and was big for his age, a lot bigger than me. After seeing the draw, I walked around the courts to see if I could see him hitting to get a look at his game in preparation for the match.

I saw him on one of the frontcourts on the lower block. I almost didn't recognize him at first because he had grown. He still had the same smooth swings. In the juniors, growth spurts could drastically improve our game due to increased strength, creating improved power and control. However, growth spurts could also be a problem if they only involved height and not weight, as was the case with me.

Another interesting point that I learned that day is that when we watch tennis, the ball seems to travel so much faster when we're standing to the side of the ball. When we are behind the ball, it doesn't seem like it's coming that fast. So I was watching this guy from the side, thinking I was in tons of trouble. Later that morning, as the warm-up got underway for our match, I kept thinking about how good this guy looked. I don't think he missed a ball throughout the whole warm-up. I tried a high ball, but it didn't seem to bother him. I tried a low slice, but it didn't seem to bother him. I was in trouble; at least I thought I was.

The match got underway, and somehow I was able to sneak out a win in the first game after several tough points. Then I sneaked out another win, and then another. At first I thought I was just getting lucky and he would make a run at me. I just kept trying to keep the momentum going. It wasn't until I had won the first set 6–0 (I am a slow learner) that I realized this guy looked like a million dollars in practice but didn't know how to keep more than two or three balls in the court under pressure. I won the match 6–0, 6–0 (we always remember these matches) and learned a valuable lesson: great-looking strokes don't mean anything if we don't know where to hit the ball.

Another experience happened to me about two years later in Austria. I was on the pro tour at the time, and the schedule allowed for my team to play a tournament in a small town in between the tournaments in the pro circuit schedule. The tournament was on slow red clay, a surface I had never played on. I didn't bother looking at the draw to see whom I was playing; I obviously didn't know anyone other than my teammates.

I met my opponent when I went to the tournament office to get the balls and the court assignment for the match. This guy carried only two rackets in his hand and had clay-stained socks. I was carrying my racket bag with six rackets in it, plus every other piece of equipment I might need during the course of a match. I admit that I thought I was pretty cool at the time. I thought this would be a good first-round match to get used to the clay. As the match commenced, things didn't go well from the beginning.

I hit what I thought was a strong serve to one side of the court and followed it with a solid volley to the other corner, and then . . . I stood and watched this guy run from one side of the court to the other, get his feet set, and make a passing shot wherever he wanted to. Clay is a very slow surface, and European red clay is extra slow, annoyingly so. The slower the courts, the more we have to think and have a game plan.

The faster the courts, the more power becomes a predominant factor, and the less we have to think (although the combination of both is optimal on all surfaces). I thought I knew how to play tennis, but with each passing game going against me, my ego was taking a huge hit. I didn't know how to deal with the situation at all. Embarrassingly, about an hour later, I had lost 6–0, 6–0 for the first and only time in my life. Another lesson learned. This guy didn't look good, but he knew what he was doing on those slow red clay courts. The physical side of performance is important, but the mental side—decision making—is everything.

A few years ago, the BYU women's tennis team was strong, but so was the University of New Mexico's, one of our toughest rivals. The two teams had been closely ranked throughout the season, with our ranking about ten spots higher. Toward the end of the season, we played them at home, so with the higher ranking and the home-court advantage, we thought the odds would be in our favor. It was a cold, windy, miserable day. From the start, our players did not appear to be into the match at all; a couple of players were even whining and complaining.

We had been having a successful year because of our emphasis on good decision making and not beating up on ourselves. We ended up losing the match 2–5. It wasn't losing the match that bothered me, but rather how we lost it. Our efforts and attitudes were appalling. I took the team indoors for a post-match evaluation. I asked the team what they thought of their performance, as I always do. Nobody said anything for a while. When I didn't let them off the hook by giving my thoughts and continued to wait for someone to say something, one of the players had the guts to say that she thought everyone played hard.

I looked at my assistant coach without saying anything, the irritation rising inside of me. She gave me a look that seemed to reflect my feelings. I then turned to the player who had made the comment and in an extremely assertive tone said, "Really!" The tension escalated. Finally, our senior and number-one player spoke up and admitted she hadn't really tried because she was so frustrated with the weather.

After her brave account, a couple of others spoke up. I thought the key element here was that the players needed to take responsibility for their state of mind and not blame others or make lame excuses or try to sugarcoat things. I wasn't mad after the players on the team took responsibility for their performances, but neither was I going to reinforce their poor efforts. After matches we usually get a good meal, win or lose. After this effort I told them I would take them to a certain fast-food restaurant, but that was it.

No one was interested. I did feel that the coaches gave everything they could, performing as well as possible, so I took them to an above-average restaurant for a nice meal. The point was made, and the team learned that if they give their best and take responsibility, good things happen; if they feel sorry for themselves and give up, they have to suffer the consequences.

A couple of weeks later, we were going into the conference tournament as the number-two seed behind New Mexico. We performed well and made it to the finals, where we were to play New Mexico for the championship. The lineups were the same at every position as they had been only a few weeks earlier at home. Things did not start well; we lost the doubles point (as we had done earlier in the year). I noticed after losing the doubles point that New Mexico was extremely excited. I remembered from one of my classes that overarousal can lead to poor concentration, making good decision making difficult.

New Mexico had never won a tournament conference title before, and it was looking more and more like today was going to be their day. After the doubles finished, there was a ten-minute period to prepare before the six singles matches went out on the court. As the team went onto the court and started their warm-up for singles, our opponents' arousal level still seemed very high.

I told my assistant coach that I thought we should keep things very simple in an effort to keep our errors down and maintain good court position. Maybe if we played assertively with fewer mistakes, they would make mistakes and essentially give the match to us. My assistant and I ran to each court to talk to our players about what we wanted them to do. As the matches got underway, four of the six players were able to execute their game plans, jumping out to great starts.

Our opponents on the two courts where we didn't get off to great starts were far more under control mentally and emotionally than their teammates. It is not surprising that these two players were New Mexico's best players. Although our players played well on these courts, they lost the first sets. However, on courts three to six we won the first sets easily. We won 6–2, 6–1, 6–3, and 6–4, respectively. Keep in mind, we had won only two matches against this team at home three weeks before, and both of these matches were long three-setters.

With our emphasis on making good decisions, we played very steady, strong tennis. Within a very short period of time for a championship match, we had won on courts three, four, and six. On court three we won 6–2, 6–1. On court four we won 6–1, 6–0, and on court six we won 6–4, 6–0. Momentum had swung drastically in our favor—all due to good decision making. Now up 3–1, we needed just one more match to clinch the tournament championship.

On court five we had won the first set 6–3, were up 2–0 in the second set, and were executing great decision making, when our player (I will call her Ruth) got a little overconfident. Translation: her ego got the better of her. This is something we are all susceptible to. When we make good decisions, we make fewer mistakes; this prompts greater assertiveness, and results in a higher level of performance and more wins. The key to maintaining high levels of performance is maintaining self-discipline, staying focused on good decision making, and not letting our egos get in the way.

At 6–3, 2–0, love up, with our opponent's father showing all sorts of negative body language, Ruth decided to deviate from the game plan. Her plan had been to hit her big forehand inside out to her opponent's backhand, burying her in the corner of the court. When she got the short ball, Ruth was to go back inside her opponent as the opponent was fast and moved to the open court quickly. Going in behind her opponent would sometimes require having to hit one or two volleys to finish the point, but it never opened the court up, minimizing Ruth's greatest weakness, her court coverage.

At 6–3, 2–0, Ruth again hit a couple of strong off-forehands to her opponent's backhand, backing her into the corner again. This time when Ruth got the short ball, she hit it down the line with the shorter distance; and with her opponent about ready to quit, it was a clean winner, 15–love. On the surface it appeared to be a great shot, but what a casual observer may not have noticed is, the New Mexico player could have gotten to it had she tried.

On the next point, the same situation developed, and again Ruth went down the line of the short ball and again she won the point. This time her opponent got to the ball but missed the pass. What I noticed was that her pass would have been a clean winner had she cleared the net. By going down the line off the short ball, Ruth was opening up the court. The down-the-line shot off the short ball was a quick and easy way to win a point, but it had a high risk to it. It is decisions like this in our lives that we need to be careful of.

The choice to take the quick and easy path appears on the surface to make life easier, but really it only exposes us to more problems than we realize. The choice to take the sure road appears tough and a lot of work but doesn't expose us to unnecessary challenges.

Up 30–love now, Ruth again hit another ball down the line, and again her opponent missed the pass, this time wide. Ruth was now up 6–3, 2–0 and 40–love and was enjoying proving me wrong. I started to wonder if she could keep getting lucky long enough that this might actually work. From the moment I had that thought, Ruth lost the next five points in a row: the first two points she watched her opponent make the passes that she had narrowly missed earlier.

On the changeover I reiterated the importance of good decision making and sticking to the plan. I admit I was pretty frustrated with her at the time; I could smell victory and was annoyed at the loss of focus. It was at this point that I made a critical error in judgment. I was overly assertive (to say the least) at expressing my expectation of what I thought the right game plan (decision making) was. When I look back with wiser eyes (hindsight is great, isn't it?) I should have portrayed relaxed body language and helped Ruth refocus on what to do instead of focusing on what not to do. But I didn't, and from this point on, Ruth was so uptight she couldn't relax and execute her game plan.

To make matters worse, her opponent sensed the fear in Ruth's body language, giving her renewed determination. She fought back with renewed strength. An hour and a half later, we lost this match in three sets. At this point in the match, I thought I had blown it. At high levels of performance, we may only get one chance, and if we are not ready for these moments, they may pass us by.

As this match was decided, I made my way up to court one, which was situated at such a position that I could not see what was going on from courts three to six. We had lost on court two to a very strong player, making the match tied at 3–3. As I walked up to court one, I was hoping that we were still in the match and had a chance. When I got there, our number-one player (Beth) was tied at 4–4 in the third set. Court one was positioned at this particular facility in such a way that a strong wind was blowing down the court and into the face of our player.

Beth was a tall, slender girl who succeeded through good decision making and great mobility, not brute strength. I wouldn't hesitate to say that Beth, at the time, was one of the weaker ball strikers on our team. She always had tape on her fingers to protect the raw skin that comes from miss-hitting the ball consistently. On the other end of the court, New Mexico's number-one player was a tremendous ball striker. I had been impressed with the skill level of this individual the whole time she was at New Mexico.

So there we were with New Mexico's extremely talented number-one player serving at 4–4 in the third set with a strong wind at her back, two games away from clinching the match and the conference title. She was hitting her serves down at Beth like missiles, and Beth could barely get the return back over the net. If Beth was lucky enough to get it back over the net, the New Mexico player would step up and smack a winner. There were no rallies. I thought to myself, "We are in trouble. Big trouble." After Beth lost the first two points without the slightest bit of resistance, something happened that shocked me.

On the third point, New Mexico's player hit another missile serve. Beth barely got the ball over the net, and then unexpectedly, the New Mexico girl missed a put-away. I couldn't believe it. Despite having all the physical talent in the world, this player was surprisingly a little unsure of herself. This went on for what seemed like an eternity. Beth would barely get the ball over the net, and her opponent would either hit a winner or miss.

It kept going back and forth, deuce–ad, deuce–ad, deuce–ad, for about fifteen to twenty (I am not exaggerating) deuces. Beth finally got game point and her opponent double-faulted, giving us, or rather Beth, the game. We were now up 5–4 with the wind at our back, serving for the match and title. In this particular situation, I took over coaching on the court. I normally would not, as our assistant was a fantastic coach. I don't know why I did in this situation but I did. I don't think we would have said anything different; in fact, I went over what my assistant had told me had been working, nothing different.

Beth attempted to execute the plan with a strong wind at her back. She had to be careful; if she lifted the ball slightly too high, the wind would get behind it and take the ball long. Hence, any sort of hesitation would ruin any plan, even a well-thought-out one. As the first point got underway, I was surprised to witness a rally. We hadn't seen one for fifteen or more minutes. Beth played within herself, executing her plan with fearless precision. This is no easy feat under this kind of pressure.

Not only were both teams surrounding the court cheering wildly after each point, but this was the final of the Mountain West Conference collegiate tournament. It was hosted in San Diego, a hotbed for tennis, so there were a lot of fans in attendance.

Beth got up 40–15 playing mistake-free, assertive tennis. On the first match point, she worked the point until she got her short ball exactly as planned, hit a solid approach shot across court, and followed it into the net. This is a great position to be in—it put all the pressure on her opponent. For a brief moment, I thought we had it, until our opponent hit the most amazing passing shot to stay in the match.

Not taking the first opportunity to close out the match only increased the anxiety. Feeling the importance of closing out the match, from the side of the court I tried to reinforce what I thought Beth should do on the next match point as she walked by me. Beth respectfully communicated to me that she was good and had it under control.

On the second championship point, Beth again worked the point, making solid decisions. She again got a short ball, but this time she stepped up and changed direction, hitting it down the line. This change of direction is normally a higher risk, but sometimes doing something that is low percentage is a good decision for no reason other than it is so unexpected.

She ended hitting a winner to win the match and the championship for us! I have always found this approach to be incredibly beneficial. Make good, reliable decisions, time after time, grinding it out so to speak. Then, when you are in those moments that come every now and then, tweak your strategy and change it up.

I have found time and time again that looking to change it up in those intense pressure situations helps athletes to stay fearless and helps them perpetuate playing to win. It also seems to work well because an opponent at this point is expecting the solid, high-percentage decision. They are not expecting a change at this point, and that is when we change it: when they are least expecting it.

The celebrations started. It is immensely enjoyable to see individuals who have worked so hard reap the fruits of their labors. I do not think it matters whether it is a tennis match, a business deal, a big sale, or witnessing our children accomplish a specific feat; the greater the sacrifice, the greater the joy.

Warning: risk taking—making decisions that are low percentage—on a consistent basis can and usually does result in inconsistent performances. I do believe high performance requires risk taking, but only at the right time and usually only when we have put the groundwork in first.

Notes
1. Favorite saying of Barry Phillips-Moore, author's professional tennis coach.

Leveraging Strengths and Weaknesses

"Seek ye first the good things of the mind: all other things shall be given unto you, or the want of them shall not be felt."

—Sir Francis Bacon[1]

As WE BECOME CONFIDENT AND COMPETENT at executing fundamentals, the next level of performance involves molding our strengths and weaknesses into our strategic plan. This involves tweaking our plan of action around our greatest strengths while minimizing (hiding) our weaknesses. As has been mentioned, growth is accelerated when we learn from the things we do well. While it is important to learn from our weaknesses and make them stronger, it is not always wise to think that our weaknesses will become our greatest strengths.

A friend of mine who has been coaching on the professional tennis tour for many years once said to me, "I am working with Ferraris and Porsches; I just need to fine-tune the engines." What he meant was that he was working with high-performing individuals, and it was not his job to rebuild the car. He just needed to find ways to fine-tune the engine to get every last bit of efficiency from it. This friend was very good at helping players find their greatest strengths, tweaking their strategic plan around their strengths and taking their level of performance to greater heights. He once took a player that had no singles ranking to the top fifty in the world in a short period of time—pretty impressive.

Another guy I knew growing up, Pat Rafter, made it to twenty-five in the world by his early twenties. Once he reached the top twenty-five in the world, he stayed there for a couple years. One summer I was coming back from Australia after the break when I ran into a man I knew from my younger days playing on the tour. He was working closely with Pat and shared some insights with me.

Pat had been around twenty-five in the world for the past two years and had even held the fastest serve in the world at one point at 133 mph. Pat and his coaches felt that while his serve was a real strength, his volleys were his greatest strength, so they tweaked his strategic plan, working with him on hitting his serve with more spin to increase control and accuracy. This allowed Pat to make more first serves, and the extra spin allowed him to get a step closer to the net for his first volley, magnifying his greatest strength.

Most would think that such an adjustment would be trivial, but at high levels of performance, a small tweak can mean the difference between good and great. After this adjustment, Pat went on a tear. He won numerous tournaments, including back-to-back U.S. Open titles climaxing at reaching the number-one ranking in the world for a brief period of time. Although Pat didn't stay at number-one for long, he still was the best tennis player in the world for a period, and no one can ever take that away. Injuries, unfortunately, shortened his career; but still, going from number twenty-five to number one was achieved by simply making a small adjustment to his strategic plan to magnify his greatest strength! High performance is all in the details.

Notes
1. Francis Bacon, *The Advancement of Learning*, Book II (New York: Macmillan, 1895), 162.

Finding the Zone

"Take the first step in faith. You don't have to see the whole staircase, just take the first step."

—Martin Luther King Jr.[1]

FINDING THE ZONE, AS PAT DID, is something we all seek. But so many of us jump over the zone and make changes when tweaking is needed. We think that extremes are the answer to high performance rather than finding the right balance from one moment to the next. By definition, change is "to make or become different."[2] Of course changes need to be made at the beginning or even the intermediate level. But at the elite, high-performing level, changing something usually means changing what made us good in the first place.

At high levels of performance, we don't need to change things, but we do need to tweak things. To tweak means "to improve (a mechanism or system) by making fine adjustments to it."[3] Balance is the key to high performance, and balance lives in the middle. Being extreme is not where the zone is. I have seen this over and over again with my athlete clients. They consistently overshoot the mark.

Here are some examples. I worked with a man named Ron on the U.S. Ski Team. He was training ten sessions a week and wanted to taper down leading into competition, so he decided to drop his training to five sessions a week. But then he felt like he wasn't doing enough and was losing some of his discipline on the skills he had spent all summer perfecting. After talking with him, I got him to compromise and do seven sessions a week. He agreed that if he felt good, he would do eight sessions, or if he felt tired, he would do six.

The biggest point I was trying to get through was to stay attentive to how he felt from one moment to the next and make good decisions—tweak his approach depending on each situation. He had a great season, and his performance improved dramatically. Obviously, there were a lot more variables involved in his improved performances—his work ethic, great coaching, and so forth—but from a mental standpoint, his balance played a greater role.

This approach fits perfectly with the research connected with high performance. Although we need to have a system to what we are doing, we also need to tweak things within that system to account for the changing variables around us. If we don't, we will fall out of the zone. So many athletes, businesses, and individuals spend their lives jumping from extremes, consistently making changes and never really finding themselves or their zone.

If only they could take a step back and see that the zone is right in front of them. Just a little tweak and they would find that balance, that momentum that can take them further than they ever imagined. This principle applies to most everything. Get plenty of sleep, but don't sleep too much. Spend money to grow or enjoy life, but don't spend too much. Take a risk, but don't take too big a risk or too many. Stand up for yourself, but don't fight every fight. Eat good food, but treat yourself every now and then. Exercise regularly to lessen the chance of health issues, but don't overexercise, or it might create health issues. The list goes on and on.

There is another point about tweaking that is worth noting. We need to be careful of superstitions that prevent us from finding the zone. For example, so many of us want to change our workouts from, say, ten hours to eight. But ten to eight may be too big of a jump, depending on your skills. What is wrong with nine or even nine and a half? Remember, high performance is all in the details. Give up on superstitions and address each situation on its merits. Systems are important because they free up energy to be channeled in more productive ways. Never underestimate the power of good decision making.

Notes
1. thinkexist.com.
2. *The New Oxford American Dictionary*, s.v. "Change."
3. Ibid., s.v. "Tweak."

The Highest Level

"You are only as good as the decisions that you make."
　　—Author unknown

THE HIGHEST LEVEL OF PERFORMANCE OCCURS when we have a clear understanding of what we are trying to accomplish and have a plan of action to achieve it. We have then developed and refined the fundamental skill sets needed. We know our strengths and weaknesses and are completely comfortable with who we are and how to maximize our strengths while minimizing our weaknesses.

Finally, at that point we have disciplined our minds to stay attentive to the present, providing ourselves with the capacity to process large amounts of information at incredible speeds, allowing for split-second decision making with minimal hesitation and doubt.

The Power of
Decision Making

"In the long run, the sword is always beaten by the mind."
—Napoleon Bonaparte[1]

HERE IS AN EXAMPLE OF HUMAN performance from two perspectives. The first perspective is a low-performing individual, and the second perspective is a high-performing individual. I will use tennis again to show the application of what I am explaining. John is an ego-oriented individual who defines his self-worth by outcomes. His only objective is to win.

Pete, on the other hand, is task oriented. His primary objective is to get better. Pete wants to win as well but understands that to win over the long haul, to win more than his fair share, he needs to focus his attention on getting better. Hence, Pete channels his energy toward the tasks that he needs to perform in order to improve his performances.

Both John and Pete have the basic strategy to hit a couple of balls crosscourt until they get a short ball; then they want to approach down the line and follow their approach shot into the net and finish the point with a volley. Note that most ego-oriented individuals would probably not have a strategic plan, but let's give John the benefit of the doubt. John executes a fundamental point doing what he sets out to do, hitting the ball crosscourt until he gets a short ball, then approaching down the line and following the ball into the net. However, his opponent (let's call him Lleyton) is faster than the average tennis player.

As John hits his approach shot and follows it to the net, Lleyton

155

gets to the ball faster than expected—giving him more choices, because John is not all the way into the net; Lleyton hits a passing shot crosscourt for the easy winner. John, having lost the point and having not achieved his objective of winning, throws an adult tantrum, yelling and banging his racket on the ground. After this brief outburst, John proceeds to get ready for the next point, still dwelling on the last point (the past).

What has John learned from the last point? Nothing. Absolutely nothing. John was so preoccupied with the outcome that he didn't learn anything. He is highly likely to keep doing the same unproductive things. Further, another interesting point is that John actually did what he planned to do. He hit the ball crosscourt until he got a short ball, approached and followed his shot into the net, yet he was mad that he did not win the point. Who was he mad at? Himself? He did what he planned to do. Was he mad at his opponent, Lleyton, for hitting a good shot? That seems incredibly unreasonable. So who was he mad at?

The object point here is that John will not improve his performance in any significant manner. Instead, he will continue to swim around in self-destructive cycles of mediocrity. It is that simple. Without growth we cannot achieve high performance.

Now let's take a look at the second perspective. Pete, our task-oriented example, is also playing Lleyton. Remember that Lleyton is very fast. Pete wants to win the match, but this objective is secondary to his primary objective of getting better. Pete has a specific plan that channels his attention to the details of what he wants to accomplish in his attempt to achieve his objectives.

His plan is first to hit hard crosscourt until he gets a short ball, step up to the short ball, approach down the line, and get in tight on the net to cut off any passing shots. Pete executes his plan well, hitting a couple of strong crosscourts, forcing a weaker short ball. He then approaches down the line and gets in a step past the service line, closing off the down-the-line passing shot.

However, Lleyton gets to the ball more quickly than Pete predicted and makes his passing shot crosscourt before Pete can get in tight enough to cut off the crosscourt pass. Pete, unlike John, has trained his mind to evaluate the reality of the situation with firmness. Pete's balanced perspective helps him learn and grow from each situation.

As Pete walks back to prepare for the next point, rather than direct his attention toward what went wrong, he first goes over what he did well: "I hit two or three strong balls crosscourt," "I got the short ball and hit it down the line," and "I got into the net tight"—all skills that he set out to achieve. Now Pete asks himself, "What can I do better next time?" He thinks, "Lleyton is fast, faster than most players. I need to get him farther off the court before coming into the net so that he cannot set his feet and have so many choices."

Pete now lets go of the past, trusts that he has learned something from it, and refocuses on the present in preparation for what lies ahead. He plays the next point, hitting hard several strong crosscourts while waiting for another short ball. This time, when he gets the short ball, he hits it back farther crosscourt, taking Lleyton farther off the court. Now Pete gets an even shorter ball to approach the net, which he does, enabling him to get in closer to the net than before. He has the down-the-line pass covered so Lleyton has to go crosscourt again. This time he cannot get as much behind the shot because his feet were not as firmly set as previously.

His pass is weak and falls low to Pete's feet. Pete hits the volley off of his shoelaces and decides to go down the line, forcing him to hit it over the higher part of the net. Thus, Pete floats the volley slightly, making the ball sit up a little. Lleyton, being the mover that he is, cuts out of the corner, gets to Pete's volley easily, and makes another pass crosscourt before Pete can get back. Again Pete loses the point. But he is better; by one shot he is better and closer to achieving his objectives. As Pete walks back for the next point, he again goes over what worked (strong crosscourts, taking Lleyton farther off the court to get the extra shot and making Lleyton hit one more ball). He again thinks, "What can I do better next time?"

Pete thinks to himself, "Lleyton is fast and cuts out of the corner quickly. Maybe if I volley it behind him, he will be heading in the wrong direction and won't be able to get back for the pass. Also, the net is lower, so I can get behind my volley more." As we can see, Pete is alert to the reality of the moment and is not afraid of the future. High-performing individuals enjoy tweaking things in the attempt to get better. They love the battle of overcoming challenges.

Pete plays the next point, again waiting for the extra short ball before approaching down the line and heading into the net. He again gets in tight, closing off the down-the-line passing shot. Lleyton goes crosscourt on his attempted passing shot but doesn't get much on it. This time Pete volleys back behind Lleyton. Lleyton, cutting out of the corner, cannot change direction quickly enough to get back to the ball, and Pete wins the point. Pete celebrates for a brief moment the joy of overcoming another challenge. He then goes over three things that went well, and one thing he wants to do better. It is a never-ending approach that accelerates growth at amazing rates.

This example applies to all areas of our lives, because it doesn't matter what the physical setting is; it is our mental approach to what we do that determines how successful and happy we feel, and whether we continually learn from what we do well and what we can do better, channeling all our energy toward controlling what we have control over. It is through taking responsibility for the decisions that we make and learning to control those aspects of our composition (spiritual, emotional, mental, and physical) that we develop a fearless mind.

With a fearless mind it is only a matter of time before we find the path to what we seek. Once on the path, the joy of continual growth, of self-mastery, begins; and when it ends . . . I don't know. I don't know if it ever ends, and I don't care, because I love the journey.

Becoming Fearless—A great benefit to using the Mental Skills Journal is that it provides feedback on the day's performance, on the day's decisions. The greatest key to achieving your objectives is to learn from your previous performance accomplishments and make an active commitment to do something different the following day. Utilizing the journal allows you to see how your choices impact your performance.

Note

1. Elie Faure, *Napoleon*, translated by Jeffery E. Jeffery (New York:

Closing Remarks

"One who fears the future, who fears failure, limits his activities. Failure is only the opportunity more intelligently to begin again. There is no disgrace in honest failure; there is disgrace in fearing to fail. What is past is useful only as it suggests ways and means for progress."

—Henry Ford[1]

THE ATHLETE, THE BUSINESSPERSON, THE PARENT—THESE individuals who achieve their objectives, who make their dreams come true, who self-actualize, who find their personal legends—all have surprisingly similar thought processes. These high-performing individuals are motivated to perfect the task at hand; their focus is on what they need to do and not on what is wrong or what could go wrong. They have a strong approach-tendency to life, playing the game of life to win in contrast to playing to not lose.

High-performing individuals direct their efforts to contributing to the greater good. They are intensely aware of what they are doing at all times, giving them a greater sense of control and confidence over their lives. Being motivated by the task at hand keeps the high-performing individual humble, sustaining a deep confidence over long periods—providing a sense of security not often seen in our modern society.

High-performing individuals have mastered the art of balance. They understand that the zone is not about more or less but about the right amount. Because their focus is tuned to the task at hand, their attention is consistently directed toward the present. Living in the present is one of the most, if not the most, important mental skill an individual can learn. It provides great feelings of control. It allows the individual to learn from the past and to leave behind any hurt feelings, reducing feelings of repression. It also prevents fear from factoring into the everyday processing of information. When the mind stays attentive to the task, the proverbial door to fear stays closed, as all fear exists only in the future.

This fearless attitude enables high-performing individuals to truly think for themselves, to trust their inner feelings, providing the necessary mental framework to feel their way through performances rather than think their way through performances. High-performing individuals trust themselves; they are less likely to seek approval from others; they are more likely to set goals that are task oriented, fostering those mental skills.

Just as poor mental skills compound to make things worse, good mental skills build on one another, fostering confidence. There are many mental pathways to performance but only one pathway to high performance—the fearless path.

Notes
1. Henry Ford, *My Life and Work* (Garden City, NY: Doubleday, 1922), 273.

About the Author

Photo by Lauren Spencer

Dr. CRAIG MANNING IS A RARE SPORTS psychology consultant. His training incorporates multiple backgrounds that have provided a wealth of knowledge and understanding to the various components that lead to high performance. Dr. Manning has played tennis at both the collegiate and pro levels; he has coached a BYU's Division 1 tennis program—building it into a national top twenty program—and has studied at one of the elite doctoral programs in the country. These qualifications are unique to the field, giving Dr. Manning experience in the highest level of performance from the perspective of a player, coach, and doctor of philosophy.

Dr. Manning earned his bachelor's degree (1995) and master's degree (2000) in psychology from Brigham Young University and a doctorate in sports psychology (2006) from the University of Utah.

His thesis examined the attributions of athletes across all sports. Two publications resulted from this study.

During the late eighties, Dr. Manning traveled the world playing on the professional tennis tour as an amateur. He traveled, practiced, and played with many of the world's top professionals, including Pat Rafter and Wayne Arthurs, while traveling to places such as France, Belgium, Germany, Switzerland, Austria, Hungry, and Holland. Dr. Manning then went on to play Division 1 collegiate tennis at Brigham Young University.

Upon completion of his eligibility, Dr. Manning was hired on as a full-time assistant coach at BYU. After four years as an assistant coach (two years with the men's program and two years with the women's program), Dr. Manning was selected as the head coach for the Brigham Young University women's tennis team. At the time Craig become one of the youngest Division 1 head coaches in the country. In ten years as head coach, the BYU women's tennis team has won four Mountain West Conference titles. Dr. Manning has been honored with the Mountain West Conference coach of the year award three times (2001, 2005, 2007), and also received the NCAA regional coach of the year award in 2005.

Dr. Manning enjoys spending time with his family, playing tennis, watching movies, and the continual pursuit of truth. He is married to the former McKenzie Baird, and they have four children who are the light of his life.

You can learn more about him at www.visualizeone.com.

0 26575 53962 2